ALL SOCIETIES DIE

ALL SOCIETIES DIE

How to Keep Hope Alive

SAMUEL COHN

CORNELL UNIVERSITY PRESS
ITHACA AND LONDON

First published 2021 by Cornell University Press

Printed in the United States of America

Library of Congress Cataloging-in-Publication Data

Names: Cohn, Samuel, 1954– author.
Title: All societies die : how to keep hope alive / Samuel Cohn.
Description: Ithaca [New York] : Cornell University Press, 2021. |
    Includes bibliographical references and index.
Identifiers: LCCN 2020039255 (print) | LCCN 2020039256 (ebook) |
    ISBN 9781501755903 (hardcover) | ISBN 9781501755910 (ebook) |
    ISBN 9781501755927 (pdf)
Subjects: LCSH: Regression (Civilization) | Social stability. |
    Social change.
Classification: LCC CB151 .C57 2021 (print) | LCC CB151 (ebook) |
    DDC 306—dc23
LC record available at https://lccn.loc.gov/2020039255
LC ebook record available at https://lccn.loc.gov/2020039256

To Daisaku Ikeda,
Distinguished Philosopher of Happiness and Progress

Contents

ALL SOCIETIES DIE

Chapter 1

All Societies Die

All societies die. We like to pretend they don't. We also like to pretend that we as individuals aren't going to die either. But no human being lives forever. Neither do societies, empires, or civilizations.

How long will our current civilization live? By historical comparative standards, European-American civilization is middle aged. One can get a sense of the life spans of civilizations by seeing how long other civilizations survived. Table 1.1 shows how long some of the great societies of the past were able to maintain themselves.

If you look at the Roman Empire, the Byzantine Empire, the various dynasties of China, and the Old, Middle, and New Kingdoms of Egypt, these empires lasted an average of a little over 550 years. Rome had a long life at about nine hundred years. China has been doing well since AD 979, with several consecutive dynasties being essentially prosperous. There was a collapse in 1911 with the onset of the Chinese Revolution, but otherwise "Modern" China had a life of over nine hundred years.

Table 1.1. The life spans of great historical civilizations

Civilization	Dates	Life span
Rome	389 BC–AD 476	865 years
Byzantium	AD 700–1453	753 years
China: Shang dynasty	1500–1300 BC	200 years
China: Zhou dynasties	1045–403 BC	642 years
China: Qin/Han dynasties	256 BC–AD 222	478 years
China: Tang dynasty	AD 618–907	289 years
Modern preindustrial China:Song/Liao, Southern Song, Yuan, Ming, Qing dynasties	AD 979–1912	933 years
Egypt: Old Kingdom	2920–2134 BC	786 years
Egypt: Middle Kingdom	2040–1640 BC	400 years
Egypt: New Kingdom	1550–1077 BC	483 years
AVERAGE		562 years
Modern Western European–American world system	1350/1492–?	500–700 years so far

Other empires were not so lucky. Byzantium had only five hundred years of true independence. In its last few hundred years of existence, it was dominated by the Italians. The Shang dynasty of China ran only two hundred years. Neither the Middle nor the New Kingdom of Egypt survived five hundred years. There were flash-in-the-pan empires, like Alexander the Great's, which collapsed soon after the death of Alexander himself.

Where do we stand in all of this? Modern Western civilization dates from the end of the Middle Ages. There was a steady process of economic and technological growth, which gave us our current high standard of living. If one dates this transition from the onset of European world dominance—Christopher Columbus's discovery of America—we are approximately five hundred years old. I take the economic growth of the fourteenth and fifteenth centuries seriously. So, I would date the modern world system from 1350, making us 650–700 years old. That would give us the average length of age of an empire when it falls—although many empires last much longer.

The experiences of other empires would suggest that the West should expect a life of no more than five hundred to eight hundred years, with a chance of an earlier extinction. The eight hundred figure is very optimistic.

What does the death of a society or civilization mean? The fall of the Roman Empire led to the Middle Ages. In China, the collapses at the end of dynasties are known as "Warring States" periods. The periods between Egyptian kingdoms were chaotic.

All of the following things have occurred during feudal chaotic periods:

1. *Standards of living collapse.* Under the empire, trade is possible. Under the empire, there is a market demand for goods and services at least in the capital city and often in the outlying territories as well. This all dries up when military chaos makes trade no longer possible. Commerce disappears. Manufacturing disappears. Food supplies dry up. The world sinks into poverty.

2. *Technology disappears.* We currently live in a world where technology just keeps getting better and better. Do you have an incurable disease now? Don't lose hope! In ten or twenty years, someone might invent something that will fix you. But there is no sacred rule that scientific skills improve all by themselves. Sometimes technology stagnates. Sometimes there is outright technological loss as the skills needed to manufacture vital products becomes lost.

   Imagine you live in some sort of postnuclear devastated world. Do you know how to make antibiotics? Could you build an electrical generator? Would you know how to drill for petroleum?

   Science is hard. Most people struggle with their math or chemistry classes. It is difficult to reproduce each new generation of scientists, engineers, and technicians on which our world depends.

3. *Crime, warfare, and violence increase.* Large secure states mean peace and rule of law within their boundaries. When the state collapses, criminals and invaders run wild.

   Rome was not a tranquil place. It had its civil wars. But during the peaceful years, which were most of them, the roads were patrolled. Invasions affected the frontiers but not the heart of the empire.

   In medieval Europe, a state could be the size of a handful of counties. Wars between microlords were endemic. Pirates ruled the oceans. There were raids from barbarians or from stronger geopolitical powers in Spain or Turkey. In that era, there was no calling the police or calling in the National Guard. If there were thieves or invaders, individual farmers had to defend themselves.

Societal death is grim. It is also inevitable. But this doesn't mean death has to come soon. Under ideal circumstances, the European-American world system could last for several centuries more.

But if we want our current civilization to live, it helps to know what exactly kills societies, empires, and civilizations. We need to know how to keep our societies alive. You cannot keep your own society alive if you do not know what kills societies in general.

Chapter 2

Is a Fall Really a Fall?

How bad is it for a society to fall? After all, Rome fell; the Egyptian kingdoms fell; various Chinese dynasties fell. But ultimately those places recovered. Currently the world is enjoying a higher level of prosperity and technological sophistication. That includes Italy, Egypt, and China.

There is even a contrarian line of scholarship that claims Rome did not really fall. To be sure, a region that was once governed by Italians came to be governed by Germanic tribes. The contrarians claim the rise of the Goths meant personal liberation and freedom, while nothing else really changed.

I disagree with the contrarians. Falls of nations and empires really are falls. In the case of Rome, all evidence suggests there was a dramatic reduction in economic activity and standards of living.

One simple indicator of how much wealth people had is the quantity of pottery remains. Pottery is more useful than other material indicators. Wood and clothing rot over time. Gold and silver are often melted and reused. Pottery lasts forever, at least as shards. Households during the Roman Empire had lots of pottery. After the fall, the number of shards drops dramatically.

Another indicator of economic activity is coinage. Gold and silver coins are relatively plentiful during the Roman Empire. They are much rarer in the 500–800s.

Populations were smaller after the fall of the Roman Empire. One can assess this by looking at the number and size of houses and calculating the likely numbers of occupants. Some of the population loss may have come from warfare or from an increase in plagues. Warfare and epidemics produce one-shot crisis reductions in population size. Reductions in food supply produce enduring high mortality and population shrinkage. Poverty and malnutrition may have easily contributed to the population shrinkage in Europe.

Why did the economy decline?

Trade collapsed after the fall of the Roman Empire. Empires served the function of reducing brigandage within their borders. Under conditions of minimal government, long-distance trade was extremely dangerous: highway robbers ruled the road, and pirates ruled the sea. In a world of rampant poverty, merchant caravans and fleets were tempting targets. Trade was only possible when empires enforced law and order on the roads and seas. Safety was a necessary precondition for long-distance commerce. Long-distance commerce made export agriculture and manufacture possible.

Warfare was not good for standards of living either. The stealing of crops and draft animals and the burning of houses severely set back capital accumulation. Standards of living fell far further in the European portion of the former Roman Empire than they did in the parts of the former Roman Empire that were in North Africa. Medieval Europe was racked by warfare. North Africa was relatively quiet.

Science and technology declined after Rome fell. The Romans had built roads that could last for one thousand years and aqueducts that could take water from the Alps to the city of Rome. No such great works were constructed between AD 500 and 1000.

Architecture and church building suffered. Christians had built large churches under the Roman Empire, but these became much smaller after Rome fell. The great Gothic cathedrals that would represent the high point of medieval architecture would not be built until the 1200–1600s, nearly a millennium after the fall of Rome.

Literacy declined as well but never completely disappeared. Some people continued to be able to read—notably members of the Christian clergy. However, artifacts with writing are much more common during the Roman Empire than they are afterward.

Not all declines and falls last as long as did the European Middle Ages. Some dynastic changes just lead to a few centuries of warfare before another hegemonic empire reestablishes itself. The Chinese Warring States period after the fall of the Zhou dynasty lasted about 250 years.

It is possible to imagine a huge spectacular catastrophe—possibly linked to nuclear weapons or an ecological disaster.

However, the most likely form of societal decline that we would see would be slow and steady deterioration. This is what occurred both in Rome and in Byzantium. Rome was sacked three times before the Western Roman Empire officially fell. Constantinople was sacked in 1204, with Byzantium surviving until 1453. However, the economy of Rome steadily deteriorated from the 200s into the Middle Ages; the Byzantine economy of the 1300s and 1400s was decadent. No one was as rich as they used to be. The skilled trades deteriorated from a lack of business. Personal security ebbed.

We assume gross domestic product (GDP) always goes up. But there is no law that says GDP cannot go down. The economy sinks into recession and then into depression and stays that way.

There is also no law that says technological skills and educational capacities cannot be lost. Much of classical Greek and Roman learning was forgotten during the Middle Ages and had to be rediscovered during the Renaissance. Science is difficult. Think of the problems we all have learning calculus or organic chemistry. Imagine a dramatic worsening of the quality of educational institutions. Even if textbooks with all the old technology are sitting happily in libraries, a general reduction in training levels can lead to society-wide reductions in overall competence and an inability to execute complex projects requiring lots and lots of skilled labor.

The future dystopia might not be a Stone Age. But it could easily be a world of poverty, marginality, and crime. It could be a world where nothing works. A world where organized gangs and corrupt officials rule. A world where incompetence is everywhere. A world where hatred and suspicion are widespread. A world where ethnic hostility and communal violence are facts of life. A world where ecological challenges are not dealt with because no one has the administrative capacity to deal with them. A world of high mortality because the medical system no longer works. A world where the standard of living is half what it is now.

No smoking ruins.

But, yes, widespread misery that endures for centuries and centuries.[1]

---

1. There are some advanced social scientists who question whether the concept of society is even useful. This is called the unit of analysis problem in both macrosociology and global history. If this problem interests you, see the appendix, "Unit of Analysis Issues in Comparative Social Science."

Chapter 3

The Fall of the Byzantine Empire

The Greatest Story You've Never Heard

When people tell decline-and-fall stories, they discuss the fall of the Roman Empire.

There are a million different versions of the fall of the Roman Empire. People invoke loss of moral will to fight, absence of technical innovation, deforestation, the use of lead pots, and many other factors.

Fall of Rome stories provide only half the picture. They talk about the Western Empire—the part ruled by Italy—which fell in 476. They ignore the Eastern Empire, what we call Byzantium, which was based in Constantinople. Byzantium lasted much longer than Rome: it survived until 1453. After Rome had completely collapsed, Byzantium was a center of power, prosperity, and culture. There was a rough period in the 600s and 700s, when it was victimized by barbarian invasion, but it recovered well. At its height in 1050, it reached from Southern Italy to Syria. It had a common legal and monetary system. Educational attainment was high, and nearly a third of the population was literate. This was higher than the literacy rate of eighteenth-century France or that of the great dynasties of China. Numeracy was widespread. They built aqueducts and functioning clocks. Their silks were highly regarded. Their mosaics and religious art were magnificent.

Byzantium had natural economic advantages. The Byzantines inherited the Roman educational system and preserved Roman engineering skills. This made them skilled manufacturers. Byzantium included Greece, long a center of shipbuilding technology and sophisticated trade. The combination of manufacturing know-how and commercial acumen produced lucrative pottery, glass, and silk industries that could sell goods throughout the Eastern Mediterranean.

Economic power led to military power, which led to ever-increasing cumulative advantage. A strong navy protected Byzantine merchants from piracy. Stable power also allowed for the creation of a stable monetary system backed by the good faith and name of the Byzantine emperor. Systematic laws and the availability of courts guaranteed the enforceability of commercial contracts.

Byzantine treasuries were full, and this money was plowed back into the economy. The state was a freewheeling, free-spending consumer. The government built monumental structures, ports, and aqueducts and supported the Orthodox Church. Its military campaigns provided substantial employment to soldiers, sailors, weapon makers, shipbuilders, and fort builders. Byzantium grew in no small measure from government expenditure, a policy we would now call Keynesian expansion.

The Byzantine Empire at its height, from the eighth to the tenth century, was remarkably egalitarian. The state went to great lengths to eliminate poverty, to protect workers, and to prevent the creation of oligarchs and plutocrats. Wealthy farmers were legally prevented from exploiting the misfortunes of their poorer neighbors by acquiring land at "fire sale" prices. Any land sales from poor to rich at "distress" prices would be voided by Byzantine judges. The purchase money went back from the wealthy landowner to the poor farmer who had been the original seller.

Urban merchants and workers were also protected. All goods in Constantinople had to be sold at a fixed margin over cost. With fixed profit margins and no competition, merchants never went out of business.

The working class was protected by welfare, job security, and legally mandated wages. The government bought grain in years with good harvests, and sold grain in years of bad harvests, keeping the food supply stable. Guilds were strong and supported by the government. They set wage rates and determined who could do what job. Employers were kept weak relative to the guilds by only being allowed to hire workers from one guild. Fixed profits and strong guilds probably led to inefficiency. This type of regulation keeps prices high and productivity low. But at the time, it kept the population of Constantinople economically secure. Standards of living were essentially maintained by law. For a few centuries, it worked. Remember, a few centuries is a very long time.

Economic growth produced military power, allowing the Byzantines to raise huge armies. Military power also produced economic growth. Part of the financing of the Byzantine Empire came through conquest. Wars were speculative profit-maximizing endeavors. To be sure, war was expensive. One had to pay soldiers and pay for weaponry, armor, ships, and fortifications. But if Byzantium won, it could loot and ravish the conquered territory. The stolen goods were used to pay the soldiers or make grants to the generals. Whatever was left paid the expenses of the imperial treasury and provided a greater tax base for future endeavors.

The actual resources that were conquered were useful. Obtaining land for farming was not that important, since you could just as easily get more land by clearing wilderness. Precious metals, ports, and skilled artisans were another matter altogether. Gold and silver mines produced the stuff of money. In the absence of financial notes or other forms of credit, actual hard currency was the only way to increase a nation's money supply.

Ports were valuable since both Byzantium and its rivals worked under the logic of mercantilism. Whoever controlled a port gave 100 percent of the trade to its own nationals. Military control of a port opened up whole territories to Byzantines and closed access to everybody else.

Artisans and skilled workers could also be conquered. Acquiring a city with craftsmen was lucrative. Corinth, for example, provided a steady output of silk goods, highly decorated glazed pottery, and glass for both the mass-produced and the elite markets. (Elite glass was often trimmed with gold.) Silk goods were expensive, so much so that they were the basis of diplomatic gifts and barter. The skilled workers who made these items could be moved to other areas. The Byzantines routinely moved conquered workers with useful skills to cities in the interior of the empire. Such relocation put their manufacturing under safe imperial control and guaranteed the emperor would get his share of the proceeds.

Using this system, Byzantium prospered mightily, notably between 800 and 1025. But then things began to fall apart. What went wrong?

Chapter 4

The End Comes to Byzantium

However, not all wars were victories, and not all military campaigns paid for themselves. Previously, the emperor didn't have to pay nobles to get them to fight. He would give the nobles conquered land plus whatever they could loot. When Byzantium lost, none of that was possible. Now the emperor had to find some other way to pay for military and governmental expenses. The Byzantine Empire crested and began to fade under the rule of Basil II.

Basil's innovation was to give the nobles tax relief rather than direct payment. He also got them to fight "for free" by letting them take land from smaller peasants. Social equality had been a key feature of Byzantine society on the upswing. Now the plan was to create nobles with vast estates and regular farmers who would have little.

Promising nobles permanent tax relief mortgaged the future to meet the expenses of the present. Future wars would have to be financed with a dwindling rather than increasing economic base.

Increasing the size of nobles' estates increased the power of regional aristocrats. This gave them independent power bases, which increased their capacity to hold back resources from future wars—or to try to take over the empire for themselves. Civil wars and regional uprisings flourished. A particularly nasty civil war between 1341 and 1354 gutted Byzantium's military strength and led to gains by the Serbs, the Venetians, and the Genoese.

Basil II favored both slavery and discouraging small farmers from becoming independent owners. He intentionally moved farmers from estate to estate to prevent them from developing legal claims on their land. He undid the policy of "no fire sale" land transfers. As land tenure became more and more insecure, the motivations for small holders to invest in capital improvements were reduced. In theory, this could have been counteracted by large farmers investing in improving the productivity of their large estates. While some of this did happen, in general, there were few returns to scale in growing olives or wheat or in raising sheep. Land concentration simply reduced the number of farmers willing to make or capable of making agricultural improvements. The increase in slavery reduced local demand for manufactured products. Free-owning farmers had disposable cash income that could be used to purchase the products of local industry. Slaves by definition had no disposable income. The creation of an underclass reduced the capacity of Byzantine nationals to buy Byzantine products.

This made manufacturers increasingly dependent on foreign sales. Because lower tax revenues were reducing Byzantium's military effectiveness as well, the adverse commercial settlements resulting from Byzantium's military defeats reduced the export market just as internal poverty was reducing the size of the domestic market. Byzantine artisans and craftsmen faced a market that was at best stagnant, and at worst in steep decline.

Constantinople fell in 1204. Although the city itself was later retaken, the economic functionality of the empire never came back. With reduced tax collection came reduced infrastructure and reduced capacity to patrol the high seas against piracy. Raids along the border increased. Critical mines were lost to enemy powers. Money became cheapened, with ever-decreasing amounts of gold and silver content. Weights and measures became nonstandard, increasing the amount of commercial fraud.

With military loss came Venetian and Genoan economic dominance. The latest pottery technology involved using alum to make advanced ceramic glazes. But once alum mines that had been Byzantine fell into Italian hands, the Byzantine potters were out of business.

The Venetians came to dominate the once-great Byzantine glass industry as well. The Venetians banned imports into Venice of finished glass, permitting only imports of Byzantine raw material. In contrast, the Venetians were selling glassware by the thousands in the former Byzantium, imports that the Byzantines were helpless to stop. With complete Italian domination of both the popular and the elite glass markets, the Byzantine glass industry practically disappeared.

The Italians banned the import of finished Byzantine silk—and ultimately took over the Byzantine-Greek cities where the silk was made. The Greek textile studios all closed. Local observers despaired of the collapse of traditional Byzantine manufactures. The philosopher George Gemistos Plethon noted,

> It is a great evil for a society which produces wool, silk, linen, cotton to be unable to fashion these into garments and instead to wear the clothes fashioned beyond the Ionian sea in wool produced in the Atlantic.

With warfare and economic dislocation came plague. Warfare promoted disease through the presence of festering corpses. Economic dislocation promoted disease by weakening the population through malnutrition. Pestilence was both a literal and an economic kiss of death. Plague concentrated in the cities, where population density and poor sanitation produced mass contagion. Given the absence of antibiotics, the only practical response to an epidemic was abandoning the plague city. Between death and out-migration, the Byzantine cities shrank dramatically. Constantinople shrank from four hundred thousand at the end of the tenth century to fifty thousand in 1423. With the abandonment of urban settlement came the abandonment of urban occupations, urban skills, and urban technology. Of all the trades that had thrived in the Byzantine heyday, only pottery and mosaic work survived. Some vestiges of commerce survived. Some locals allied with the Venetians or the Genoans, representing those interests in Turkey or abroad. Italy was willing to purchase a few Byzantine raw materials, such as foodstuffs and dyes.

While Constantinople did not disappear entirely, Byzantium did. The egalitarian society, the mass literacy, the popular standards of living, and the local arts and sciences all disappeared. The region was conquered politically by the Ottomans, economically by the Italians. Byzantium went from being a center of power, wealth, and culture to being a subordinate outpost of an Atlantic economy. Much of its fall was of its own making.

Chapter 5

THE ENVIRONMENTAL CAUSES
OF VIOLENCE IN THE MIDDLE EAST

Socially destructive forces are not just something that occurs "in history."

Currently, there is terrorism, warlord violence, and ethnic conflict through-out the Middle East and the belt of land immediately under the Saharan desert. Some people attribute this to Islam, but that would be a mistake. There are many peaceful Islamic nations, such as Morocco, Malaysia, and Azerbaijan. These places are pro-Western, are feminist, and abhor violence.

People forget the more obvious characteristic of the Middle East. The Middle East is a desert. The desert is expanding. The desert is destroying the semiarid lands next to the desert. As this happens, local residents are thrown into economic desperation.

Why is the desert expanding? The population is increasing.

The semiarid lands next to the desert are fragile. The semiarid has tenu-ous water supplies. It supports only low scrubby vegetation. Agriculture is marginal. The population essentially survives on herding.

When the population goes up, the size of the herds goes up. The animals overgraze and destroy the vegetation. When the vegetation is gone, the land no longer supports water. The plants never grow back, and the land turns into a desert.

Between 1948 and 1962 and again between 1990 and 2004, 1.6 million square kilometers of semiarid land converted to fully arid desert. This reflects a global drying of the earth in which 4.6 million square kilometers of land have transformed into drier formats while only 1.98 million square kilometers have from irrigation or natural sources transformed into wetter sources. The amount of land being reclaimed in moister systems is less than half the amount of dry land that is being newly created.

Maps 1 and 2 are physical maps of the terrains of Africa, the Saudi peninsula, and the Middle East. The dark areas are the semiarid. These contain a substantial percentage of the conflict and civil wars of the world. Northern Nigeria is the center of Boko Haram. Chad produced the mercenaries used by Muʿammar Muḥammad al-Gadhafi to bolster his regime. Sudan and Southern Sudan include the war in Darfur, the war between Sudan and Southern Sudan, and the civil war between the Dinka and the Nuer. Eritrea fights with Ethiopia. Somalia has the armed warlords who fight over Mogadishu, and the pirates who attack shipping off the Horn of Africa. The semiarid in the Arabian Peninsula contains the only area of ongoing civil war and terrorism: Yemen. In the Middle East, the western band of the semiarid includes Eastern Syria and Western Iraq. This is the primary field of activity of ISIS. Farther east in the semiarid is Kurdland with Kurdish-Turkish wars and the mercenaries who fight ISIS. The semiarid continues into Western Afghanistan, where it occupies the primary centers of activity of the Taliban.

In all of these settings, people are turning to warfare because normal economic life is no longer viable. People are living in a desert with no way to support themselves. If they move to the city, their options do not become dramatically better. They are farmers and herders with few urban skills. They arrive with no money, so they live in the slums. They have neither education nor skills nor cash. The slums are already filled with other unemployed people due to the weak economic performance associated with rentier states. The migrants become landless workers who have lost everything.

Dying farms, dying towns, widespread unemployment, and huge numbers of idle marginalized youth lead to many of the responses that produce joining terrorist organizations. What do people in the Global South do when they cannot get a job and cannot economically survive?

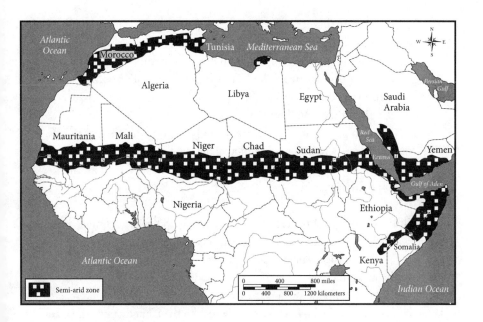

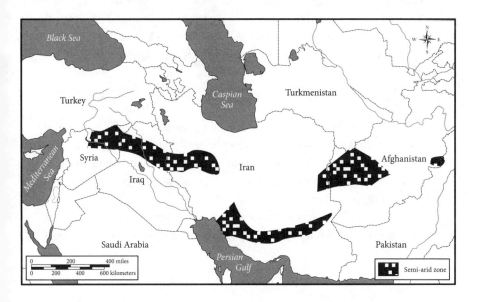

1. They can turn to crime. Poverty makes some people more predatory and violent than they would otherwise choose to be.
2. They can go to work for a local politician or warlord. Politicians and warlords are always looking for help, and they always have funds to pay their supporters. Poverty makes some people more partisan than they would otherwise be.
3. They can go to school. Educational opportunities for the poor are often extremely limited. Religious schooling may be the only feasible choice. Poverty makes some people more religious than they would otherwise be.

This is the power of the terrorist organizations. They are criminal gangs *and* warlord organizations *and* religious education organizations all at once. They cover all of the avenues taken by people who would otherwise be economically marginalized.

Having no economic prospects can result in despair that would lead to someone being willing to put on a suicide vest. In the United States and Canada, it is not uncommon for gang members to throw themselves into violence knowing full well they are likely to die themselves in a few years. If you see no future for yourself, and you see no future for anyone around you, that is even more reason to decide to go out in a blaze of glory. At least this way you will make an impact on the world.

∽

It is entirely possible that the world will end because of an ecological catastrophe. Certainly, such things have happened before. However, we also need to think about the effect of ecological loss on people's willingness to work together. We need to think about the ecological causes of people taking up arms against each other.

It is hard to create sustainable development in a war zone.

It is hard to be green in a world where the dominant color is the red of freshly shed blood.

Chapter 6

THE FRENCH REVOLUTION

Fighting about Taxes at the Worst Possible Time

The causes of the French Revolution, and there were many, are well understood. Scholars have written thousands and thousands of pages on the subject. There is one point about which nearly all scholars agree: in the months before each revolution, the French king was in deep financial distress.

Readers who are social scientists will recognize the argument that is about to be presented here as that of Theda Skocpol in her *State and Social Revolution*. That book is revered as a classic in sociology. In 1979 it won the prestigious C. Wright Mills Award. Among professional French historians, there is a mix of admiration for the book and concern that Skocpol omits various additional factors. However, no one in any discipline disputes the basic fact that the French monarchy was facing acute financial crises.

What was the problem? It was not that Louis XVI was particularly wasteful, although he had a lavish lifestyle at Versailles.

The issue was instead one of crushing military necessity. France, being a geopolitical power, had no choice but to fight wars. France was surrounded by England, Spain, and Prussia, all of which had expansionary dreams.

Fending off these enemies would become more expensive every decade. The rise of new industrial technology meant the perpetual rise of better cannons, better rifles, better ships, and better fortifications. Economic development and population growth meant that armies and navies were getting larger and larger. This put increasing pressure on the treasury. The War of the Austrian Succession in the 1740s was about 25 percent more expensive than the previous War of the Spanish Succession in the 1700s. The Seven Years' War of the late 1750s was 50 percent more expensive than the War of the Spanish Succession. The war of the American Revolution in the 1770s came at a discount because it was nearly entirely naval. Before the revolution, France was dealing with invasion threats from Spain and England and was spending over twice as much as had been spent on the Seven Years' War.

So, France was preparing for an unavoidable double war with England and Spain. The government was broke. The disputes within the elite about who was going to come up with the money to pay for extra military expenses led to revolution.

France was fiscally crippled by the fact that a substantial proportion of its financial base was exempt from paying taxes. The Catholic Church was exempt from paying taxes due to its status as the state religion. Much of the nobility was exempt—often as the result of having received a substantive or ceremonial position that came with special taxation privileges. The tax collectors themselves were exempt from taxation. A variety of merchant and industrial groups had special tax concessions. The French elite fragmented into dozens of small factions—all attempting to ensure their own small group would remain tax exempt. When peasants and radical workers rose up in what might otherwise have been a small and easily containable rebellion, the noble factions and the branches of the armed forces linked to those factions could not agree on a common response. The revolutionaries found divided conservative forces, as well as members of the elite willing to oppose the king if this would help them win their battles about future tax obligations. The result was the overthrow of the king and the entire noble class.

To be sure, taxes were not the whole story. There was the example of the recent successful American revolution, and new ideas about democracy and freedom. There was a rising capitalist middle class resentful of the superior status of the aristocracy. The new bourgeoisie had aspirations of obtaining land currently owned by the nobility and the church and was hostile to traditional legal protections of peasants and workers. There was a rising radicalized, educated, skilled working class hostile to all elites, noble, capitalist, or religious. There was a traditional peasant class, although to be sure, many of their complaints were about taxes.

That said, it is hard for a nation to maintain itself as a geopolitical power in the face of an elite class or a general population that does not want to pay for military expenses. If internal divisions caused by other factors are intensified by a tax war, the consequences can be dramatic.

Chapter 7

How States Actually Die

The Real-Life Death of Somalia

It is hard to study societal death using modern societies, because most of those have not fallen yet.

There is a modern state that did fall. The state that died? Somalia. After the government of Siad Barre was overthrown in 1991, Somalia became genuinely stateless. There simply was no government. Individual regions were ruled by loose coalitions of clans. The capital, Mogadishu, was divided between two warring subclans. The economy tanked, falling by 22 percent between 1991 and 2001. The country fell into civil war. In the 1990s, thirty thousand Somalis died on the battlefield. A further three hundred thousand died of starvation and famine-related diseases. Terrorist movements began to form. The coastal populations turned to piracy. There were almost no pirates in Somalia under Siad Barre. In 2008, there were fifteen hundred.

The Somali government fell in part because the economy was fragile and social cohesion was fragile. Most modern industrial nations have a far more robust social fabric than Somalia did when it fell into trouble.

Somalia is extremely barren. A majority of the land does not support agriculture. Over 50 percent of Somalis are pastoralists (herders) because farming is just not viable in much of Somalia. Somalia has a higher percentage of pastoralists than any other nation in Africa.

Herding is not good for social unity or cohesion. It promotes isolation and mutual hostility. This is especially the case for barren land such as that in Somalia. Because of the low carrying capacity of the soil, the herding population has to disperse itself widely in order to avoid overgrazing. Dispersal means people live in isolated family units. Clans need relatively little from other clans. They compete over resources such as pasturage and water. There is little one clan can do to help another. As a result, Somalis have very small webs of cooperation. Family members can be trusted. Non–family members are viewed with indifference or suspicion. This is an open invitation to conflict.

British and Italian colonialists exploited this tendency. They armed rival families and encouraged clan warfare as a strategy of divide-and-rule. Winners got better land and access to state power. Losers did not disappear. Mutual suspicion and animosity increased.

The colonial powers created various Somali governments. (Borders changed over time.) They created elites to administer these. The elites turned predatory quickly.

Governing Somali regions was nearly impossible. The economies were so minimal that they produced nowhere near the taxable surplus needed to finance a modern administration. Most governments survive on their nation's resources—which they tax. Somalia never could since there was never enough to tax. The absolute scarcity of local revenue meant the Somali government was from the outset entirely dependent on foreign subsidy. This meant handouts from the colonial powers in the early twentieth century. This meant foreign aid or military assistance from the United States or the Union of Soviet Socialist Republics (USSR) in the late twentieth century.

Compared with the dismal prospects of the Somali economy, the aid money from Washington or Moscow was a bonanza. Everyone was trying to get a piece of it. People wanted government jobs. Salaries were ridiculously high. Corruption ruled. Being in the government was the difference between abject poverty and lavish wealth.

Bad behavior by the state elite was motivated in part by the fact that good behavior probably would not have accomplished much. The Somali bureaucrats were technically demoralized. Developing the economy was a dismal prospect. Banana plantations existed in the south of the country; they survived only because Italian colonialists banned non-Somali bananas from entering Italy. The country's geopolitical prospects were weak. Somalia's sparse population made it a poor prospect as a military power. Somalia did not win a single war in which it engaged. Without local revenues, the foreign aid money was hardly sufficient to build a complete network of schools or a viable public health system.

Conceivably, Somalia could have maintained a status quo as a low-expenditure, low-performance ministate. But that was not to be. The general noncooperation of Somali clans with their clan neighbors translated into national noncooperation between Somalia and its neighboring nations.

With limited resources, there was not much an idealistic civil servant could do. Plus, there was no activity in the economy even remotely as lucrative as getting one's share of the foreign monies in the government budget.

Or it was for a while.

The money that was not dissipated in salaries or embezzlement was poured into military expansion. The elites invested in armies to protect their own access to public funds. The general suspiciousness associated with mutually noncooperative dispersed clans turned into a foreign policy of national antagonism. Somalia was one of the few African nations utterly opposed to Pan-Africanism. Somalia was publicly hostile to every single one of its neighboring nations.

This led to both border raids and major warfare. War was doubly expensive for the Somalians, as there were the expenses of not only recruiting soldiers but also arming them. Wars resulted in major dislocations of civilian populations, leading to the necessity of maintaining large refugee camps. Often, the government of Somalia was supporting a population of displaced persons equal to 40 percent of its normal population.

Remember, there was no economic surplus to pay for all this. Massive government spending on wars, refugees, and corruption without an economic base led to hyperinflation. For most of the 1980s the inflation rate was at least 50 percent, with spikes up to 200 percent. The civil servants suffered the consequences of their actions. Hyperinflation made their salaries worthless. By the late 1980s, a monthly government salary provided only three days' worth of actual living expenses. Once government salaries became worthless, government employees stopped coming to work. The Somali government simply stopped functioning.

Chapter 8

SOMALIA AFTER THE FALL

The process of government death in Somalia was not bloodless.

As conditions got worse, there was increased political dissent. The government responded to dissent with an iron fist. Following the model of the Italian fascists who had governed Southern Somalia historically, the government tried to crush the opposition with all-out destruction. Opposition clans had their wells poisoned and their herds slaughtered. Because the Mogadishu elite was very small, and most regions were in rebellion, nearly every clan was forced to defend itself against the Mogadishu government. So the entire country armed itself in self-defense.

This widespread mobilization was enough to force Siad Barre from power. However, the opposition was too divided to create a new administration. The whole country splintered along clan lines. The result was a Hobbesian war of all against all.

The collapse of a functioning Somali state also meant the collapse of the Somali navy. This is what led to the rise of Somali piracy. Unlike the pastoralists, fishermen on the Red Sea or Indian Ocean coasts were peaceful and nonconflictual. There was no need to fight over grazing land or wells. There were plenty of fish in the ocean for everyone. Coastal villagers generally got along. This changed after the Somali navy collapsed. With no coast guard, there was no one to protect Somali waters against foreign fishing boats. The Somali fishers were small-time operators. The foreign fleets were larger ships, generally from Korea or Yemen. The Somali fishers had to drive off the intruders themselves. This meant learning how to approach a larger ship with a series of small ships and use small arms and semiautomatic weapons to get the foreigners to leave. Once these skills were acquired, Somali flotillas could think about engaging larger and larger targets. With no police to stop them, the vigilantes turned into kidnappers. The pirates learned how to attack oil tankers and get the very large ransoms that oil companies would pay to get their valuable ships back.

The social conditions producing piracy did not improve. To the extent that the problem was resolved, it was resolved though international cooperation at a global scale. Naval escorts were organized using the combined naval forces of the United States, India, Pakistan, Russia, China, Iran, the European Union (EU), Canada, and Australia. Note the joint presence of several geopolitical rivals—both the United States and Russia, both Russia and China, both the United States and Iran, both India and Pakistan. Kenya and Yemen do not patrol, but they provide courts and prison facilities for captured pirates. Clans fight clans and produce piracy. Nations cooperate with nations and produce peaceful international trade.

The civil war continues in Somalia as of 2020. Over a thousand civilians die each year. There are over 2.6 million internally displaced refugees. Much of the fighting is between a somewhat restored government and a terrorist group, Al-Shabaab. Interclan violence exists as well. Modest economic growth and some government functioning have returned to Somalia. But its overall prospects are as weak as ever.

～

There are ties among the fall of Somalia, the fall of Byzantium, the rise of Middle Eastern terrorism, and the French Revolution. The contexts and issues are different, but there are key unifying themes.

What do these four very different stories tell us about the causes of societal death?

Chapter 9

What Links These Stories?

Ancient Byzantium. Contemporary Northern Nigeria. Contemporary Eastern Syria. The French Revolution. Modern-day Somalia. All of these were very different cases. Things fell apart in each setting for distinctive reasons, many of which were local.

However, there are common threads that unite the various disaster stories:

1. *Cooperation helps. Factionalism and infighting hurt.*

    The French aristocracy doomed itself by splintering while arguing over which subset of nobles would have to pay the new taxes.

    Somalia nailed itself multiple times by factionalism. Interclan divisions prevented the Somalians from developing a unified response to defend themselves against British or Italian colonizers. Clan divisions led to various civil wars, all of which wreaked mayhem on the country. The Somali government's preference for fighting with neighbors forced it to spend money on armaments rather than development and led it to fight losing wars that led to refugee crises.

Note also that Somalian piracy was put to an end when the other nations of the world banded together to ensure maritime safety near the Horn of Africa. Even rivals such as the United States and Iran put aside their differences to unite against the pirate threat.

2. *Governments don't survive without adequate tax revenues.*

Byzantium doomed itself by granting tax subsidies to its nobility. The revenue losses from the subsidies guaranteed that, in the future, Byzantium would not have the financial resources to fight wars.

Louis XVI's inability to raise enough money for impending wars led to the calling of the Assemblé de Notables, which led to the movements for his removal.

The Somalian government was always in tenuous straits due to the lack of taxable surplus in the country. The state survived temporarily on foreign aid and military assistance from external powers. When those sources of funds were removed, the state fell.

3. *The economy matters.*

Byzantium's growth was spurred in part by generous income guarantees for Constantinople residents. When Byzantium began to lose wars, the loss of critical ports, mines, and cities with skilled artisans sent it into a permanent downward spiral.

The expansion of the desert in north-central Africa and the Middle East destroyed the livelihood of the farmers and herders who had previously lived on the semiarid. They turned to crime, warlordism, mercenary conflict, and terrorism because there were few other ways to survive.

Somalia's fundamental lack of economic growth doomed any state that attempted to rule it.

4. *Ecological preservation can be essential to economic growth.*

The destruction of the semiarid led to a parallel destruction of regional economies throughout Africa and the Middle East. The warfare that followed led to even greater economic decline. Somalia was not immune from this syndrome.

5. *Ethnic tensions inhibit rational state policy.*

The inability of African or Middle Eastern countries to prevent the loss of the semiarid came from governments paralyzed by ethnic divisions. The government of Iraq has to balance the conflicting demands of Sunnis, Shias, and Kurds. Nigeria is a petrostate and does not lack financial resources. Ecological policy in the north is often subordinated to balancing the social and economic interests of the Ibo Southeast, the Yoruba South Center, the nonarid Housa North, and the volatile dynamics of the capital city of Lagos. Somalia is no stranger to ethnic divisions.

6. *State capacity matters.*

State capacity means not only having adequate revenue but also having adequate expertise, being corruption-free, and being accepted as a legitimate authority. The Byzantine state was crippled not only by losing its autonomous financial capacity but also by having nobles who were perpetually trying to secede or grab power for themselves. Byzantium's ability to defend itself from foreign enemies was gutted by having to fight and win a series of regional uprisings. Somalia's government was crippled by widespread corruption and flagrant lack of expertise. The predatory and aggressive nature of the state elite guaranteed widespread resistance in the rest of Somali society.

These are pieces of the jigsaw puzzle that help explain how societies die. But in this fragmentary form, they do not represent a fully coherent explanation. The rest of this book is about developing a more organized, systematic treatment of the process of societal decline.

There is, however, a long tradition of decline-and-fall books, most of which take a different intellectual direction than that put forward here. Not all of those traditional specifications are helpful. Let's look at some of those competing models. We can then return to the historical record and lay out a model of societal death that is a realistic approximation of what the current industrialized world can actually expect.

The two most common end-of-the-world theories invoke ecological catastrophes and moral crises.

Chapter 10

Rethinking Ecological Catastrophe

Ecological catastrophes are not likely to be the primary cause of the collapse of our contemporary society. The primary threats are elsewhere.

This is not to say we don't have ecological problems. The danger to our planet is very real. Global warming means coastal flooding, extreme weather events, the loss of entire islands and cities, and the disruption of our food supply.

An even greater ecological problem is population growth. In theory, population growth ought to be under control. World birthrates are steadily decreasing, but the world population will continue growing throughout the entire twenty-first century. In 2100, the world will have more than one and a half times as many people as it had in 2015.

Population growth has devastating effects on the environment because natural resources do not increase at the same rate as the number of people using those resources. Population growth

1. exhausts our energy supplies,
2. uses up the supply of drinking water,

3. exhausts natural food supplies such as fish in the ocean,
4. uses up the supply of arable land for farming,
5. promotes deforestation,
6. intensifies the development of slums—with all the problems associated with concentrated poverty.

It is very easy to link such developments to the downfall of societies. There is a substantial historical and archaeological record of civilizations that have collapsed because of ecological problems.

Table 10.1 shows various ancient societies that have collapsed from ecological woes. Those are real societal deaths on the historical record.

Ecological writers note that not all environmental threats are lethal. They represent a challenge to a society. Like any other problem in life, if one adapts to a challenge, one survives. If the government, the technological system, or the economy of a society remains functional, even dire environmental threats can be addressed.

In the environmental literature, the jargonistic term for such adaptation is "ecological modernization." This refers to a society using technology or regulation to counteract or eliminate environmental threats.

There is absolutely, positively no guarantee that ecological modernization will occur. Ecological modernization is nice when it happens. Being cured of cancer is nice when it happens. Cancer often kills, and so do ecological threats.

That said, some environmental stories have happy endings. Ecological modernization occurs frequently. When the Great Lakes were becoming heavily polluted, treatment plants were built to clean water and reduce industrial waste. Laws were passed banning the dumping of toxic waste into water supplies. Over time, water quality improved, and the worst threats to the Great Lakes were averted.

Table 10.1. Societal collapses caused by ecological crises

Easter Island	Deforestation	Loss of wood for canoes
		Reduced fishing
		No forest animals for meat
Mayans	Deforestation	Erosion due to loss of ground cover
Norse Greenland	Deforestation	Loss of firewood in arctic conditions
Mesopotamia	Overpopulation	Overirrigation leading to soil salinity

The world is exhausting its supplies of petroleum. Through ecological modernization, new supplies are being discovered. Some conservation is occurring. Alternative sources of energy, such as wind and solar power, are being promoted. This is not a fully resolved problem. Fracking and nuclear power pose grim issues on their own. But we are stumbling toward some sort of progress, even though it is an imperfect progress.

Capitalism promotes ecological modernization. Modern capitalism is bizarrely capable of reproducing itself in the face of disaster. What happens when a good becomes scarce? The price goes up. This lowers the consumption of the now-scarce item. When oil prices spiked in the 1970s and 1980s, Americans really did shift toward using more fuel-efficient cars because gasoline had become more expensive.

Modern industrial societies have shown tremendous resilience in the face of all-out disaster. The Great Chicago Fire led to a tremendous boom afterward as the city physically reconstructed itself. Both Germany and Japan were nearly destroyed in World War II. This was followed by thirty-five years of prosperity as both countries rebuilt from the ground up. Rebuilding a flooded New York City in the face of global warming would be a grim process, but it would not necessarily mean an end to American or world prosperity. The economy would keep going. Real estate brokers in New Jersey and Connecticut would make a small fortune.

Ecological crises are survivable, *if* a society has the capacity to do something about them. This is a huge "if." The critical issue is often not the ecological threat itself but the societies' capacities to face any kind of problem.

Cooperation is reduced in the face of internal and external war.

Cooperation is reduced in the case of organized violence.

When everyone fears for their life, no one is working together. No one trusts the partners that will be needed to pull off the common endeavors that are the solutions to the joint problems that represent a threat to all.

Where ecological threats are truly dangerous, it is because they undercut the capacity of a society to cooperate and work together. This was illustrated by the example in chapter 5 of desertification in the Middle East. If ecological problems increase terrorism, warlordism, and organized crime, then they undercut the foundation of cooperation.

Desertification is easy to fix. You build wells that are protected from sunlight so water doesn't evaporate. You implement agricultural techniques that conserve water. You provide access to contraception to reduce the extent of population pressure on the land.

But no one is going to provide agricultural extension services or open women's health clinics in the middle of a civil war zone.

If our planet becomes barren, it may be because we were fighting too much to do anything about it.

Chapter 11

Rethinking Moral Crisis

One of the oldest tropes in the "end of the world" genre is "We are going to die because of a moral crisis." The ancestor of this argument is Edward Gibbon, author of *The History of the Decline and Fall of the Roman Empire*. Gibbon himself made many sophisticated arguments in the thousands of pages he wrote about Rome. But he is remembered for the claim that Rome became soft and decadent, given to orgies and luxurious living. The soft youth were irreligious, unpatriotic, and unwilling to fight. Rome was overwhelmed by barbarian hordes with more spartan lifestyles and greater military discipline.

Moral arguments can be made by anyone in any part of the political spectrum; they are the most common, however, among the religious right.

Consider one of the best books in the genre, *When Nations Die: Ten Warning Signs of a Culture in Crisis*, by Jim Nelson Black. Black's treatment is unusually complete and covers nearly every argument made by moral crisis authors.

He argues the following:

1. Americans are no longer safe due to high crime.
2. High crime is the result of out-of-wedlock births and general lack of moral and religious instruction.
3. Welfare creates out-of-wedlock births, which produce crime.
4. Welfare also undercuts the work ethic, leading to idle youth.
5. Religious values have been undercut by secularism, leading to a huge spiritual emptiness that people try to fill with pleasure.
6. Big government undercuts churches to pursue their own secular agendas.
7. Big government taxes the industrious rich in a wrong-headed attempt to provide welfare to the idle and morally reprobate poor.
8. Secularist vulgarism has produced violent hypersexualized mass media while eliminating the teaching of the foundations of Western culture from schools and universities.
9. Youth have become indolent because of this culture. They are less studious and more ignorant.
10. Rome fell because its youth became secularized, hedonistic, and ungrounded in traditional culture. We will fall the same way.

What's wrong with this picture?

1. Levels of criminal activity are wildly exaggerated. In the past centuries, crime has fallen rather than risen. In 2018, less than 1.2 percent of Americans were the victims of violent crime.
2. The link between moral degeneracy and military weakness is tenuous. Professional football players are often hard-drinking, hard-partying vulgarians. They would have been fearsome fighters on a Roman battlefield.
3. The size of an army is not determined by the "indolence of youth." It is determined by a government's ability to pay for soldiers and armaments. If a government can't pay its soldiers and suppliers, few will fight for it, indolent or not. Paying for soldiers requires taxation. Taxation is anathema to moral crisis authors.

4. Moral crisis authors contrast the decadent present day with a previous golden age. Golden ages were not always so golden. American traditionalists revere the frontier spirit of the American West. The Wild West was no haven of Christianity, abstemiousness, or scholarliness. The students at today's universities may be poorly informed about European culture. The telephone-booth-cramming, goldfish-swallowing fraternity boys of the 1920s were not necessarily well versed in Byron or Rousseau either. Shakespeare may have been a noble poet. But the primary entertainment near the Globe Theatre was bearbaiting. The average play on the Elizabethan South Bank was a revenge-laden bloodfest not that different from a modern horror movie.

5. Moral crisis authors bemoan the replacement of particular religions with newer ideologies of less value. New Age cults may or may not provide the same profundity or inner meaning associated with traditional religions. However, inner peace is not what allows a society to survive.

Societal survival is based on large groups of people working together to solve common problems. The largest possible web of cooperation is the human population as a whole. Identifying one group as having superior values and another group as being barbarian reduces the size of the potential web of cooperation. It is not helpful to set rich people against the "idle" poor, white people against "criminal" blacks, or Christians against "culture-destroying" vulgarians.

Moral crisis theorists worry about the Romans being overwhelmed by the Goths. In a deeper sense, why are the Romans and the Goths fighting at all? To be sure, if the Goths have declared war on the Romans, the Romans have no choice but to defend themselves. Governments ignore geopolitics at their peril. But there is no reason for Romans to be fighting Goths, Hindus to be fighting Muslims, or Shias to be fighting Sunnis. Are there not ways to identify problems of concern to groups with cultural differences and have both groups work together to find acceptable solutions?

There is one form of moral crisis theory I do like: theories that warn about the dangers of being divided from each other. Paul Collier has a nice version of such a theory in his *Future of Capitalism*. He argues that modern societies are being pulled apart by divisions between high-tech cities and older industrial areas. Yuppies live in an internationalized world—where they have more in common with techies in other countries than they do with industrial-city co-nationals. They have little interest in patriotism and little interest in the residents of "tacky" areas. The residents of frost belts have no illusions about the goodwill coming from the yuppies. The yuppies are willing to shut down the coal mines and steel mills that are the heart of the Rust Belt. Residents of older cities are willing to cut education because the new high-tech economy does little for them. The result? No one agrees on anything. Political paralysis ensues.

Theories of the superiority of Culture X over Culture Y tend to shipwreck on their own internal contradictions. Theories of unity and division can predict when people come together and cooperate. Moral crises occur when we start persecuting the bad guys for being immoral.

Chapter 12

NETWORKS OF COOPERATION

To understand how societies die, let's look at one of the greatest theories of social science. This theory provides an expansive and useful explanation of the social progress that has occurred historically. This theory has a major flaw—a problem that has been assailed constantly over the past fifty years. This problem is easy to fix. Put in the obvious patch that is needed and you have a serious model of societal death.

The supertool is Talcott Parsons's theory of social systems. Parsons was the dominant theorist in American sociology between 1930 and 1970. He was conservative, ethnocentric, naively optimistic, and an appallingly bad writer. But on the points that he was right about, he was brilliant.

He argued that all social progress comes from networks of cooperation. Parsons referred to these networks of cooperation as *systems*. He viewed systems as being analogous to the organs in a human body. Each organ makes a specialized contribution that allows the body as a whole to survive and grow. Every organ performs a unique function. The organs could not survive without the contributions made by each other. Every form of human organization takes the form of a system: A romantic couple. A family. A firm. A nation. The world.

All systems have to perform four critical functions. Parsons referred to this set of four key functions as AGIL:

A (adaptation): All systems need to get economic resources from the environment in order to survive. The body needs food and oxygen. Human societies need food, energy, and raw material. Most units need money. Adaptation usually involves subcomponents making some kind of contribution to the system either through donating resources directly or by working to make resources.

G (goal attainment): This is for all intents and purposes governance. Collective decisions have to be made as to how adaptation is to be accomplished. Goal attainment harmonizes the process and makes sure key jobs get done.

I (integration): Integration ensures that everyone on the team cooperates with the general plan. There is always the risk that some members of the system will slack off and not contribute their appropriate share. There is also the risk that there will be exploiters who rip off the system for their own gain. Integration is in essence social control, the process that protects the system against deviance.

L (latent pattern maintenance): Most effective systems do not have to coerce their members to do what needs to be done. Nor do members get paid for everything they do. Members of social groups tend to contribute and be prosocial because they believe in what they are doing; they share the ideals of the system. Latent pattern maintenance is the cultural system that imparts the values, beliefs, and ideologies that make people want to be good voluntarily. People have standards. They get these standards from parents, from peers, from schools, from religion, from mass media, and from any other institution that transmits ideas of value.

Parsons believed that systems evolve. Social progress occurs because societies make themselves better and more capable in response to threats to their well-being. They do this through a process of "homeostasis." (I warned you Parsons was a terrible writer.) The system has an ideal state that it needs to attain. There is some shock to the system that poses a threat to that ideal state.

The system adapts to that shock by reestablishing the earlier happy condition. This is how a thermostat works in your home. Is your house too cold? The thermostat turns up the heat. Too hot? The thermostat turns down the heat.

Homeostasis is often accomplished by developing distinctive institutions that specialize in solving the problem under consideration. Agriculture yields are down? Create an agriculture school. Lost a war? Build an air force or get a better network of spies. Parsons called this process of institution building "differentiation."

Parsons argued that human history consists of constant progress owing to this ever-continuing process of differentiation. Societies become more complex and specialized. Dedicated knowledge is created to solve every problem imaginable. Every component of the system contributes to the welfare of every other component. The cultural system ensures that the knowledge needed to survive will be created and that all the elements work together in a network of cooperation, with each part willing to sacrifice to ensure the preservation of the common good.

Societies need to do this in order to survive. Evolutionary pressure means the societies with the least knowledge, the least differentiation, and the smallest contributions to the system will die. Present-day societies represent the highest form of adaptation, with adaptation, goal attainment, integration, and latent pattern maintenance being at their historically highest levels of differentiation and effectiveness.

Parsons assumed that every day in every way societies just get better and better. History is a linear monotonic advance toward higher and higher levels of functionality.

This is obviously absurd. Social progress does not occur automatically. Whatever exists now is not always better than what has existed previously. Life was not better in medieval Europe than it was under the Roman Empire. Homeostatic adjustment does not mean that problems are always solved. Your body has white blood cells to protect you against infection. Sometimes bacteria kill you anyway.

But What If We Broke Parson's Assumption That Positive Evolution
Always Occurs?
What If We Ran Parsons in Reverse?
What If Societies Did Not Adapt?
What If Societies Could Not Unify around a Given Goal?

What If Unintegrated Free Agents Milked Every Opportunity
for Their Own Gain?
What If the Culture of Voluntary Cooperation Did Not Cohere?
What You Would Have If This Occurred Is Societal Decline
Leading to Possible Death.

Things would simply stop working. Large networks of cooperation would stop functioning. Common problems would not be solved.

Parsons is a theory of social progress *when social progress occurs.*

Reverse Parsons is a theory of social progress *when social progress does not occur.*

We need to take Reverse Parsons very, very seriously.

Chapter 13

WHY BIGGER IS BETTER

It is easy to understand why the world works better if people participate in networks of cooperation.

What is important for the understanding of societal life and death is that big networks of cooperation work better than small networks of cooperation. Bigger really is better.

This argument was made most forcefully by S. N. Eisenstadt, one of Parsons's best students. He studied the rise and fall of ancient empires. His finding: maintaining large size was essential. The empire finding came from his own work. The logic was Parsons all the way.

What are the advantages that large systems enjoy over small systems?

1. *Large systems have larger resource bases.* Large systems have a greater area and a bigger population. This means they draw from more physical and natural resources. They collect more money. They have more people doing more work. They can raise a larger army. This

is why China has been richer than the fragmented states of northern Europe for a larger percentage of history.

From an economic standpoint, larger systems have larger markets. This means that entrepreneurs have greater potential consumer demand and a greater potential pool of capital. Singapore and Albania are both small places. Singapore maintained extensive business networks all over Asia. Albania intentionally closed itself off from the world. Which nation became richer?

The governments of large systems can do larger, more impressive projects than can those of small systems. It took the resources of an empire to allow the Romans to build aqueducts. Large American states have better public universities than do small ones. California has the University of California at Berkeley. Texas has the University of Texas at Austin. New York State has Cornell, which is actually half-public. (You could call it the State University of New York at Ithaca.) These are among the leading research institutions in the world. The teaching at the University of Delaware and the University of Wyoming may be fine. However, these universities do not have the scale to become significant research players.

2. *Large systems can support greater specialization.* Large units have the intrinsic market to support a high level of specialization, or, as Parsons would say, differentiation. Specialists tend to be better at what they do than generalists. A small town can support a family physician. A small city can support surgeons, oncologists, and ophthalmologists. A major metropolis can support an ophthalmological practice that treats only the rare wet version of macular degeneration. If you have the rare wet version of macular degeneration, you are far more likely to get better treatment in a major metropolis than in a small town.

3. *Large systems can draw from a larger talent pool to fill positions requiring unique skills.* There are some jobs that are done better if they are staffed by a genius or a person with extraordinary talents. Lots of people want to be gymnasts. Not everyone is a Simone Biles. Lots of women want to die their hair blonde and become a star singing sexy songs. Shakira does this better than the pop wannabes. The star effect is even more important in leadership positions. Drawing

from a larger pool of talent increases the chances that one will be able to hire a Thomas Edison or a Steve Jobs or a Warren Buffett.

What does all this imply?

> *A Dyad (A Couple) Will Outperform a Single Individual*
> *A Family Will Outperform a Dyad*
> *A Tribe Will Outperform a Family*

(A "tribe" here is any group bound by a common subculture. It can be a majority ethnic group as well as a minority ethnic group. It can be a professional group. It can be a regional group. Whites, Blacks, Nigerian Americans, Harvard grads, computer programmers, Southerners, Californians, and Gulf fishermen are all tribes.)

> *A Nation Will Outperform a Tribe*
> *A Global Network Will Outperform a Nation*

Capitalism is a global network. It easily crosses national borders, organizes trade patterns, work relations, and ideology worldwide, and is amazingly robust to what governments do within it. It is one of the most effective wealth-generating mechanisms on earth.

The internet is a global network. No one nation can control it.

The world travel system is a global network. Not only are there conventions governing how planes and boats go from country to country, but there are standard rules. One example: a red light means stop and a green light means go.

Scientific research is a global network. While Americans are very active in the world of big science, global participation in this system is critical. The best scientific minds come from all over the planet—although they may work in a country other than where they were born.

One of the greatest dangers to societal functioning is a preference for small social networks over large social networks. Marriages where each partner thinks only of himself or herself and not the viability of the relationship end quickly. Married people are happier, wealthier, and live longer than divorced people. Countries that engage in regional or ethnic rivalries get consumed in internal politics.

Preferring large social networks to small ones is what led to the prosperity of Switzerland, one of the richest nations in the world. The country was originally an agricultural, mountainous economy. Its manufacturing got a jump start by offering religious asylum to Protestant craftsmen who were being persecuted in Catholic France. The artisans accepted the offer of religious toleration and started a *passementerie* industry, elaborate decorations for clothing. The engineering for the machinery used in *passementerie* evolved into the engineering for watchmaking. The legacy of offering religious toleration was that Switzerland became the world's primary watchmaker.

Swiss tolerance also allowed it to unify the country without any major disputes between French- and German-speaking areas. That same tolerance kept it out of Europe's destructive twentieth-century wars.

Prioritizing large networks of cooperation worked for the Swiss. It can work for other nations as well.

Chapter 14

LEGITIMATION

So Hard to Earn, So Precious to Have

Large systems may function better than small systems. However, having a large system is not entirely unproblematic. Large systems generate inequality. Inequality contributes to the rich and powerful treating everyone else badly. Being treated badly makes people hate the system. When the system is widely hated, no one works to preserve the system. This is how nations and empires fall. Parsons spent much of his professional career apologizing for inequality because he felt it was a necessary concomitant of system survival. This did not win him friends among progressives. But Parsons did have a reasonable point about the unsavory side of prosperity and well-being.

Why do large systems generate inequality? Half of it is bona fide returns to merit. Half of it is leverage of personal position into advantages for friends, families, and oneself.

As societies and empires get bigger and bigger there are simply bigger and more complex organizations to run. It is a lot harder to run a global agribusiness than it is to run a small farm. It is a lot harder to manage the armed forces of a major geopolitical power than it is to be a village constable. Note that because these tasks are difficult, fewer people are qualified to do them, and fewer people do them really well. Not every general is a Napoleon or a Julius Caesar. Not every businessperson is a Henry Ford or a Bill Gates. Large organizations amass large amounts of resources. The individuals who do a good job controlling that large mass of resources are rewarded for their efforts.

Not all of the rewards of the elite are based on merit. People who have access to power and money control other people's access to power and money. They want to promote their friends to positions of power? No problem. They want to promote their family to positions of power? No problem. They want to promote members of their ethnic group to positions of power? No problem. So even if the original great founders were unique, remarkably talented individuals, often the individuals who follow in their wake are not so unique and not so talented. They are, however, taking other people from other social networks and other ethnic groups and closing them out of the good positions in society. The well-connected ones enjoy the good things of life. Everyone else is on the outside looking in.

The organizations run by the elite take things from people and control their lives. The governments tax. The police departments arrest. The corporations send bills for charges due. The armies conscript. The big companies drive the small ones out of business. The schools make rules and discipline students. Religious leaders ban this and ban that. Bosses make people work hard. People have lots of reason to resent people who exclude them from opportunities, take things from them, and regulate them.

The trouble is that some of these exercises of authority are necessary for a society to function. Governments can't build schools or hospitals or provide defense against invaders unless they collect taxes. There will be a million automobile accidents if people do not obey the traffic cops. Students will not learn anything in school if they do not obey the teachers. Economic life will be in complete chaos if no one does what they are supposed to do on the job. Let's not even mention the necessity of paying bills that are owed.

Parsons argued that *legitimation* is what allows all these good things to happen. Without legitimation, society cannot exist. Legitimation is accepting the authority of someone over you as being legitimate. When you go to the doctor's office, the doctor can instruct you to remove your clothes, can perform invasive examinations, and can stick needles in you after that. You do what the doctor says because you accept the doctor's authority as being legitimate. You believe that the doctor means well and is trying to improve your health. You also believe that the doctor knows more about your health than you do. You accept the doctor's authority as being legitimate, so you voluntarily do what he or she says.

Why does legitimation occur?

In some cases, there is legitimate quid pro quo. The powers that be provide enough bona fide service that it makes sense to give them what they want.

In some cases, there is an ideological structure that teaches why submission to authority is good. Children are taught from an early age to obey their teachers and employers.

In some cases, you don't have a choice, because there is overwhelming force on the side of whoever is in charge. If there is going to be trouble unless you have a good attitude, you get a good attitude fast.

Legitimation, however, is fragile. Most good behavior and compliance with laws is voluntary. We internalize moral codes, believe we are good people, and do the right thing. But we live in a world where powerful individuals and large organizations do not always do the right thing. Seeing those examples, it is easy to lose faith.

If we get sick of it all, we don't pay our taxes, show up late for work, make junky products, and run traffic lights. We may treat our family and friends well. But the larger institutions on which everything is based stop working.

Chapter 15

Psychological Foundations of Societal Survival

The fundamental rise and fall of world systems is essentially based on economic and political considerations. There are giant global forces that make some countries rich and other countries poor. There are practical material considerations that make some countries powerful and other countries weak.

However, psychology and culture are not irrelevant. This is particularly the case on maintaining large webs of cooperation. Being in a web of cooperation implies some sense of moral obligation to help other people who are in the web. It also means a sense of obligation to protect the web as a whole. Moral obligations come from culture; they come from the transmission of ethical norms.

In the latter part of the book, after the discussion of the material factors that lead to societal decline, we discuss the psychology of survival. Individuals really can invoke culture to stem or slow a society that is on a self-destructive path.

But I will mention one key psychological attribute of survival right here. People's willingness to contribute to a web of cooperation depends on whether they consider themselves part of the web of cooperation at all.

The critical concept here is the *greater and lesser self.* This idea derives from the Japanese philosopher Daisaku Ikeda and refers to the multiple ways we think of our identity. The most orthodox definition of self is the lesser self. The lesser self is basically me, myself, and I. In microeconomics, when we talk of profit-maximizing individuals, those individuals are trying to get the most money for themselves, and to heck with everyone else. However, as the self becomes greater, we think of other people's welfare as being just as important as our own.

A mother may treat her baby's happiness as being as important as or more important than her own. She may even make sacrifices for her husband.

In economics, in the theory of the firm, all the employees of a company work to maximize the profit of the company. In the real world, not every worker puts in maximum effort for the sake of the corporate bottom line. But dedicated employees and managers who internalize the company mission and care about profitability, product quality, and the reputation of their company do exist.

Some people are patriotic and identify their nation's well-being as being as important as their own. They volunteer for military service. They make donations to political candidates. If they are public employees, they put in long hours to fulfill the mission of their particular department.

Some people see themselves as global citizens, or as parts of international networks of meaningful cooperation. They work to save the wildlife in faraway countries. They give money to victims of disasters in distant places.

The question is, Whose well-being is as important as one's own? It makes a difference if one sees oneself as white or as an American. It makes a difference if one sees oneself as an American or as a member of humanity.

The more people share a larger conception of self, the more they are willing to make the contributions that make cooperation at that larger level viable.

Chapter 16

Progress That Is Real

The Reduction of Poverty

Critical social scientists, such as me, are cynical people. The rest of this book will give the reader plenty to be cynical about. We are facing impending loss. However, to truly appreciate loss, we have to be aware of the good stuff we have in the first place.

Parsons was right. Over the long span of history, many things have improved dramatically. In the next few chapters, I discuss the obvious so as to remind people of the fat benefits that we have been enjoying. Critical commentators make devastating critiques of our world. But we make these critiques in heated, air-conditioned houses with flush toilets. We have had full meals of the foods we prefer. We are in good health with no physical pain. We own personal computers with which we can write critiques. We check the internet to keep up with our recreational lives. We will probably not be beaten, tortured, arrested, or killed for writing the things we want to write.

These benefits do not generalize to everyone in the world. Much of the world's population is poor, sick, and in great physical danger. But more of the world's people are enjoying the good things of life than has ever been the case in human history.

Over the course of history, the world has become rich. Some regions are overwhelmingly richer than others. Some of those riches are at the expense of the poorer regions. However, every region has benefited from the development process. Every part of the world is enjoying the greatest prosperity in human history.

Table 16.1 shows GDP per capita for the world as a whole and its various regions from 1820. The data come from a set of authors analyzing the Maddison data set, the best numbers we have on the level of economic development from AD 0 to the present day.

Some of those early estimates are pretty dicey. Would you believe someone who says they know the GDP of Mongolia in 355? The further back in time you go, the more the estimates of economic well-being are speculative. Scholars disagree violently on how rich China or the Mayans were relative to the Europeans—and it is hard to settle the question definitively. However, by 1820, the competing estimates tend to converge. This holds even for disputed cases such as the Ottoman Empire.

Say whatever you like about economic development from 0 to 1820.

It is quite clear that from 1820 on we have seen an extraordinary explosion of economic growth and standards of living that has benefited every region of the world. The bottom line shows that world standards of living were thirteen times higher in 2000 than they were in 1820. Imagine if you

Table 16.1. Regional GDP averages per capita, 1820–2010 (1990 purchasing parity)

	1820	1870	1950	2010
Western Europe	1,226	1,976	4,518	20,841
Eastern Europe		719	2,583	8,027
Western Offshoots	1,294	2,421	9,528	29,581
Latin America / Caribbean	595	754	2,502	7,109
East Asia	579	543	655	9,804
South / SE Asia		516	675	3,537
Mideast / North Africa	580	720	1,459	5,743
Sub-Saharan Africa			843	1,481
WORLD	**605**	**837**	**2,082**	**7,890**

Note: Western Offshoots = United States, Canada, Australia, New Zealand.

were making thirteen times more money today than you were making at some time in the past. That would unquestionably be a major improvement.

This growth occurred continuously over time. The year 1870 was better than 1820, 1950 was better than 1870, and 2000 was better than 1950.

Note that every single region of the world benefited from this growth. Even the poorest region, sub-Saharan Africa, had its income nearly double between 1950 and 2000. It is unlikely that sub-Saharan Africa was much richer in 1820 than it was in 1950 or 2000. The growth also occurred in Latin America, Eastern Europe, and Southern Asia, including nations that are known for their enormous numbers of poor people, such as India.

Now, some skilled social science readers may take exception to the use of GDP per capita statistics to measure economic well-being. They would argue—correctly—that in many developing societies, wealth is concentrated among a small elite. A country can show gigantic improvements of GDP from exporting oil or a valuable mineral, without any significant reduction in the poverty of the masses. So, in principle, all of this higher income could be retained by a small number of millionaires while starvation continues to be rampant on the streets.

Table 16.2 speaks to that objection. It measures calories consumed by the general population. The rich may be able to hog all the money and hog all the income. The rich may be able to earn one million dollars of personal income while poor people get only fifty cents of personal income. But the same statement cannot be made for food. A rich person cannot eat one million calories a day. The benefits of food are widely dispersed among the population.

Food consumption data exist for only very recent dates. However, the trend in the long-term data is clear. Food consumption has gone up substantially from 1965/1966 to 2015. Yes, the rich are eating more. They went from nearly 3,000 calories per day to 3,500 calories per day. People in the industrialized nations are getting fat.

Table 16.2. Food consumption per capita (calories per day)

	1965–1966	2015
Industrialized nations	2,947	3,500
Developing nations	2,054	2,980
WORLD	**2,358**	**3,050**

However, people in poor nations went from 2,000 calories per day to nearly 3,000 calories per day. This is the level of food consumption that the rich nations had in 1965.

So economic development appears to have at least reduced starvation and malnutrition of the poor nations of the world. People in the poor nations are better fed, and probably better off.

Do these favorable trends translate into better health?

Chapter 17

PROGRESS THAT IS REAL

The Improvement in Health

Yes, the generalized improvement in income has led to better health.

Table 17.1 shows historical trends in life expectancy at birth for various regions as they have evolved over time. Life expectancy at birth is the average number of years that people will live in the course of their lives. Most countries keep death records, which record how old the person was when he or she died. For countries that kept good statistics, our knowledge of life expectancy goes back a very long time. For countries with poor data collection capacity, we know life expectancy only for the modern era, when statistics improved.

Globally, the number of years that people live has steadily improved over time. In the 1880s, the average person lived to be only twenty-seven years old. Life expectancy improved by 1900 and again by 1950. In the 2000s, the average person lived to be sixty-nine years old. People's life spans more than doubled.

Note that this improvement occurred in every region of the world listed in the table. It occurred in every time period listed in the table. Even

Table 17.1. Historical regional averages of life expectancy at birth by decade

	World	Western Europe	Eastern Europe
1880s	**27.0**	40.4	—
1900s	**30.8**	46.3	35.8
1950s	**50.8**	68.2	62.5
2000s	**69.1**	79.7	69.1

	US, Canada, Australia, New Zealand	Latin America, Caribbean	East Asia
1880s	40.3	—	—
1900s	50.8	29.4	—
1950s	69.2	53.5	47.4
2000s	78.1	72.6	74.7

	South Asia, Southeast Asia	Middle East, North Africa	Sub-Saharan Africa
1880s	24.6	—	—
1900s	24.5	—	—
1950s	41.0	43.5	37.9
2000s	65.9	70.1	52.1

sub-Saharan Africa, which has the highest rate of mortality in the world, saw life expectancy improve by nearly one-third between the 1950s and the 2000s.

Why was life expectancy so low in 1880? A life expectancy of twenty-seven did not mean that everyone rolled over and died on their twenty-seventh birthday. The high death rates came from high rates of infant and child mortality. Before the rise of modern medicine, approximately 25 percent of babies died within the first year of life. If you survived until your first birthday, you then had a 25 percent chance of dying between then and age twenty. If you survived all that hunger and all that disease, you were likely to be one tough survivor. Thus, even without modern medicine, if you made it until age twenty, you were likely to make it until age sixty, seventy, or eighty, just as we make it till age sixty, seventy, or eighty today. The improvements we have seen have generally been improvements in pediatric health. This was enough to make a huge difference.

What improved?

The food supply improved. As more and more of the world's people became more and more nourished, their bodies became stronger and more capable of fending off disease. Mothers who were better nourished had babies with bigger birth weights, which gave the babies a higher chance of surviving.

Sanitation improved. More and more people got access to clean piped water, so their drinking water no longer carried infectious diseases. Sewerage systems were installed. Houses became equipped with flush toilets. People were no longer living next to piles of human and animal waste, which reduced their exposure to fecal bacteria.

Modern medicine improved. Antibiotics made it possible to fight infection. Surgery was invented—and surgical techniques improved. The rise of orthopedics meant that fractures no longer led to the amputation of limbs or a life spent being lame or immobilized. Diagnostic techniques improved, allowing for accurate assessments of diseases. Modern dentistry became a thing. This meant that people no longer lived with debilitating toothaches or had to undergo traumatic tooth extractions without anesthesia.

To be sure, not all diseases are curable. We have made progress against heart disease and against certain forms of cancer. But there are still diagnoses where the doctor gives you the bad news and tells you the short time you have remaining to live.

We do not live forever, but we live for a longer time. We spend a larger proportion of our lives not in pain. Mothers no longer have to go through the ordeal of seeing one-quarter of their babies die, and then one-quarter of their children die. Lives spent not mourning one's children are generally happier lives.

Not only are we in better health, but we are more secure and safe. The next chapter discusses how levels of crime have declined. We are now at less risk of dying in incidences of violence.

Chapter 18

Progress That Is Real

The Reduction of Violent Crime

Rates of violent crime have dropped dramatically over the course of the last eight hundred years. High-quality crime statistics do not exactly exist for the Middle Ages. However, we do have historical data on homicides. When there is a dead body, some official power makes note of it, even in settings with the most minimal levels of government. So, we can reconstruct the trends in homicide from about the 1200s.

Table 18.1 shows the homicide rates over time for England, the Low Countries, Scandinavia, Germany, Switzerland, and Italy. Every country tells the same story, although the timing of that story differs by nation. There was a dramatic drop in homicides from twenty-three to fifty-six homicides per one hundred thousand inhabitants in the Middle Ages to one or two homicides per one hundred thousand inhabitants in the present day. In England, the big drop occurred between the 1200s and the 1500s, when the homicide rate dropped from twenty-three to seven. By the 1700s, murder rates were nearly at their contemporary low level. Belgium and the Netherlands started the Middle Ages with a homicide rate nearly twice that of England. It took till

Table 18.1. Historical national homicide rates by period (homicides per 100,000 inhabitants)

	England	Netherlands & Belgium	Scandinavia	Germany & Switzerland	Italy
13th–14th centuries	23	47	—	37	56
15th century	(15)	45	46	16	73
16th century	7	25	21	11	47
17th century	6	8	18	7	(27)
18th century	2	6	2	7	11
19th century	2	2	1	3	13
20th century	1	1	1	1	2

Note: The twentieth-century statistics exclude 1995–2000, which were missing from the source. Figures in parentheses are missing data and have been estimated by interpolation.

the 1500s for that rate to drop. By the 1600s it was practically at the British level. Medieval Scandinavia had just as high a murder rate as the Low Countries. It was down to two homicides per one hundred thousand inhabitants by the 1700s. Germany and Switzerland closely resemble Britain, but they started from a higher level. Italy was the most violent of the Western European countries. By the 1400s, seventy-three people per one hundred thousand were being killed. Italy's rates decline over the same period as the other nations. However, because it was starting from an extraordinarily high level of violence, it took longer to get to objectively low murder rates. It achieved a homicide rate of only two per one hundred thousand in the twentieth century.

Why were crime rates so high? For starters, brigands ruled the road and pirates ruled the sea. Peasants who had little access to other resources preyed on both merchants passing through their villages and merchant ships passing on the coast.

Crime rates were also high because of violent disputes. Disagreements between people were resolved with fisticuffs. Disputes that went beyond fisticuffs turned into lasting feuds, as violent retribution was responded to with even greater violent retribution.

What improved?

1. Both the food supply and the economy improved. Quite simply, poverty causes crime. In historical periods where harvests failed and

hunger was a reality for adults and children alike, adults stole in order to feed their families.

2. Governments developed courts of law. Disputes that had previously been resolved by personal violence could now be taken to a judge for remedy. Furthermore, the presence of appropriate conflict adjudication mechanisms allowed countries to punish those who took the law into their own hands.

3. Governments developed police forces. We are used to the trope in westerns of the new sheriff cleaning up crime in the town. This happened in more places than the Wild West as the new law enforcement figures hunted down and punished criminal gangs.

4. Governments developed prisons. Chronic offenders who would not be deterred with warnings could be put behind bars, where they would be incapable of harming the general population.

5. Governments developed schools. Idle youngsters are more likely to get into trouble than older people with more responsibilities. To be sure, schools helped produce economic gains as well. Having a population with higher literacy and more skills will produce greater productivity and greater growth and prosperity. However, schools structuring the lives of children and teenagers, keeping them busy and out of trouble, significantly reduced the rate of juvenile delinquency. Sports played as big a role as Latin.

6. Fertility decreased. Beginning in the late eighteenth century, couples began to have fewer children. With smaller families, it was easier for mothers to supervise children and to maintain overall levels of discipline.

7. Travel increased. This increased the exposure of villagers to people from other regions or other countries, which led to increasing cosmopolitanism. Cosmopolitanism was particularly noticeable in cities; in the last eight hundred years, urbanization has increased markedly. Greater exposure to people from distant locations led to greater social interaction, and greater willingness to treat exotic strangers as human beings rather than as potential victims.

I give the greatest weight to economic growth. It is no accident that crime rates are greater in the Global South than in the Global North. Removing poverty removes a lot of the motivation to engage in crime.

But notice the central role of government in producing a lot of the reforms that controlled crime. Governments developed courts, police, prisons, and schools. As we shall see in later chapters, they also played a key role in stimulating economic growth.

Protecting personal security and controlling crime are fundamental components of social well-being and progress. While we value peace and the protection of individuals now, it has not always been that way. Raiding and theft were instrumental to the origins and creation of civilization as we know it. Everything we value in advanced societies has an ancient origin in coercion and violence. Controlling crime is central to the preservation of society. But the earliest societies were made by criminals.

Chapter 19

The Motivation to Not Cooperate

The Origins of Civilization in Raiding

Social cooperation is wonderful. It produces economic prosperity, longer life spans, and less crime. If this is the case, why is there so much hostility and noncooperation among nations?

The fact that working together in a system improves life does not negate the fact that the world has a lot of exploitation. There may be a lot of benefits to cooperation, but some countries benefit at the expense of others.

Growing by beggaring your neighbor is not a recent phenomenon. It goes back to the very origins of civilization. Civilization was built on the basis of raiding. The world's oldest occupation is not prostitution. The world's oldest occupation is theft.

Societies became large and wealthy when some places got military advantages over the others. Some areas were fertile. Others had good water transportation. This allowed them to have larger populations. Larger populations meant larger armies. They could raid their neighbors, stealing whatever was portable and worth having. Raiders stole animals. Raiders stole harvested crops. Raiders stole objects of beauty or value. The loot was used to pay off soldiers to motivate participation in future raids. Slowly but steadily, the militarily dominant societies became wealthy. Slowly but steadily, the militarily dominant societies evolved into empires.

A key intermediary step was the development of tribute. When societies had grossly unequal power, it was pointless for the weaker group to let itself get slaughtered. It was easier to offer in advance the goods that would be seized anyway. For the conqueror, receiving tribute was easier than fighting. Tribute evolved into taxation. The soldiers came around regularly to collect what was due. The slaughter ended. The exploitation continued.

Raiding and military conquest led to the dominance of men over women. In more egalitarian societies, such as simple hunting-and-gathering societies, gender relations were fairly equal. If women were unhappy with men, they could simply pack up and move far away from the offending male. There was little property to divide. Therefore, rigid rules of inheritance and marriage were not needed. Some conventions regarding marriage still existed; however, the preferences of the men and women involved were the primary driving force, as they are today.

Raiding led to the transformation of women into prizes of warfare. Raiding societies had always permitted victorious soldiers to loot the losing population. If the chieftain wanted a larger percentage of the economic take for himself, he had to find some other motivation for his soldiers. Soldiers were males aged thirteen to forty. Males in this age range have one thing on their mind. Allowing the soldiers to do what they wanted to the victimized female population motivated the soldiers to do a whole lot of fighting. It also freed up a share of the surplus to go to the chieftain himself.

The rise of empires and the rise of civilization were both predicated on rape.

Rape evolved into slavery. Just as the soldiers took material goods home, they took women home with them too. Soon they were taking conquered males home as well. The conquered males were put to work on unpleasant tasks that no one in the conquering society wanted to do.

This is how the system of irrigation developed. Irrigation was not the product of some great technological innovation. Anyone who has seen water flow downhill knows how irrigation works. The problem is that digging irrigation ditches is backbreaking labor. Metal was scarce in this period; it was reserved for ceremonial objects and weapons. This meant there were no metal picks or shovels. All of the ditches for irrigation systems would have been dug with wooden spades. None of the locals would have wanted that job, even if the increase in agricultural yield would have been tremendous. Slaves were the perfect workforce for this miserable task. The superior yield from irrigated crops would have led to even greater population size, which would lead to greater armies, more conquests, and more slaves.

Once you had slaves, you could build impressive buildings. Slaves could move large blocks of limestone that nobody else wanted to haul.

Conquest stimulated literacy and numeracy. Written records allowed the conquering nation to keep tabs on how much its tributary nations had paid. They also allowed for the creation of formal documents specifying the size of future obligations.

Conquest stimulated art and science. Now that large buildings could be built, architects could figure out how to build them, and sculptors and painters could figure out how to decorate them. Greater expansion of territory allowed for the greater discovery of mines. This stimulated metallurgy for the creation of weapons. Other sources of raw material became the basis for decorative glass and pottery.

Women remained under the control of men, even in settings that were no longer taking slaves per se. Warfare was the key to wealth and power. Population size was the key to having large armed forces and victorious warfare. Controlling women meant controlling fertility. Controlling fertility meant controlling the next generation of future fighters. An emperor didn't want just any man to have children. If he was disloyal or rebellious, this could lead to future political problems. If any man was going to reproduce, it was essential that he be loyal to the current regime.

So marriage and sexual contact ceased to be determined by the romantic interests of the parties involved. Women were not allowed to mate with whomever they pleased. Women's marriage partners were chosen by elders for political and economic reasons. Men who were disloyal to the current regime would be prevented from marrying. Men who were politically and militarily useful would get good brides.

So, raiding led to patriarchy.

Raiding led to the rise of taxation and the state.

Raiding led to dramatic increases in material wealth.

Raiding led to dramatic increases in artistic and scientific capacity.

Naturally, of course, this chapter exclusively refers to ancient history.

Raiding isn't important to modern economic growth, now, right?

Chapter 20

PRIMITIVE ACCUMULATION TODAY

Raiding Is Not Dead

Raiding was not only a feature of the ancient economy. It was the foundation of Western economic growth. It is an active component of economic development in the Global South today. Capitalism may operate through the voluntaristic choices of the free market. But it reinforces itself with plain, ordinary garden-variety coercion.

The technical term for modern-day raiding is "primitive accumulation," a word used by Karl Marx to describe the origin of capitalism. He was referring to an "enclosure" in eighteenth-century Britain where peasants' common lands were seized by landowners so the landowners could raise sheep. Marx was too cynical in thinking that seizing common land was the only key to Britain's economic growth. But, Marx was too naive in thinking that primitive accumulation only applied to England in the 1700s. In fact, seizure of land is the basic mechanism with which capitalism fuels its growth.

The no-duh example of capitalism based on forcible land acquisition is the United States. The United States first became rich as an agricultural power. It grew cotton in the South that it sold to England. Later, it grew grain in the Midwest that it sold throughout the world. By the 1870s and 1880s, the United States was the primary supplier of wheat and corn to the rest of the world and was a leader in both meat production and processed food.

Cotton, wheat, and corn all require land.

That land was taken away from Indians, generally by force.

The European settlers arrived on the Atlantic Seaboard. They steadily pushed west following manifest destiny until they controlled everything between the Atlantic and the Pacific.

There was nothing unusual in what the Americans did. Spanish- and Portuguese-speaking people seized all the land in Latin America. Muscovites moved east and seized the land in what is now Russia. English (and occasionally French) settlers took over Canada, Australia, New Zealand, and South Africa. In all these cases, the original people living on these lands were displaced or marginalized.

David Harvey, the Marxist geographer, has argued that what allows capitalism to survive is the repurposing of space. Geographical areas that are not producing market value are converted to a form that does produce market value. Turning frontiers into farmland or mines is one obvious example. But this occurs in urban economies too. When developers go to the edge of a city and build new housing, offices, and retail, they are commodifying space. Generally, this is done through simple market transactions. The owner of a house that is now worth twenty times its original value because the developer needs the land for a shopping center may be delighted with the windfall gain. In the Global North, these transfers are generally voluntary. People may haggle over the price, but the final deal is generally signed by willing partners.

This is not always the case in the Global South. Here, land is often just taken away by plain, ordinary coercion. India has land mafias—gangsters who are in the business of "clearing" land for development projects. In Latin America, this job is done by paramilitaries: informal squads of volunteer soldiers who do the dirty work for politically well-connected investors. Some paramilitaries have day jobs as police officers or soldiers. Others are private security personnel.

Colombia has a particularly violent history of land seizure. The most flagrant case of this was La Violencia, a ten-year civil war starting in 1948 where the government organized private militias with the explicit purpose of taking as much land as possible from opponents of the regime. The military and its allies became vastly wealthy from the giant estates created from the expropriated land. Land seizure had been common in Colombia before La Violencia and it continued unabated afterward.

Jasmin Hristov has documented much of the scale and violence of contemporary expropriation in Colombia. Here are a few of her stories.

In 1997, a paramilitary unit commanded by Rodrigo Tovar Pupo, otherwise known as Jorge 40, invaded five different villages: La Pola, Pueblo Nuevo, San Angel, Chivolo, and La Estrella. They assassinated a number of residents. They then returned to three of the villages and informed the peasants they had fifteen days to vacate their properties. They were working with the full cooperation of INCORA, the government land registry. In the next few years, INCORA revoked the land titles of the peasants in the villages because they had "abandoned" the area. The titles to the land were then transferred to members of Rodrigo Pupo's squad and to members of a parallel paramilitary organization.

In Uraba, in the 2000s, the local elite wished to set up palm oil plantations in response to declining prices in bananas and cotton. Palm oil requires different terrain than is used for the other two crops. The residents of the palm oil region were Afro-Colombians. The paramilitary chiefs were white. There commenced a series of armed assaults on Afro-Colombians, causing the residents to flee for their lives. Flight generally meant losing the title to their land. Hristov lists the various palm oil companies now active in the region. She also lists which of these are owned by paramilitary chiefs.

In Medellin, in the first ten months of 2009 alone, some fourteen hundred people were displaced by paramilitaries.

In Colombia as a whole, there were no fewer than forty-two assassinations of land rights activists between 2007 and 2011.

One can understand how someone who has been forced out of their home at gunpoint may be unenthusiastic about the government that supported the gunmen.

However, one may argue in theory that "this is the price of progress." Land acquisition leads to economic development, and economic development leads to prosperity for all, right?

But the record of the West in producing economic growth in the rest of the world is decidedly mixed. There are economic motivations for poorer nations not to be entirely enthusiastic about cooperating with the global economic system.

Chapter 21

THE MOTIVATION TO NOT COOPERATE

How Europe Historically Underdeveloped Much of the World

In theory, global webs of cooperation make all societies function better. This includes making every society richer. World trade should lead to economic development and general prosperity.

However, economic cooperation with the West has been a mixed blessing. While there have been obvious benefits from global trade, many countries in the Global South were substantially impoverished. This makes some groups legitimately suspicious of cooperation with Europe and the United States. Most Americans are unaware of this backstory, making hostility to the West seem completely baffling.

The most flagrant abuses occurred in previous centuries. Europe has not always been richer than the rest of the world. In the Middle Ages, Europe was an underdeveloped, primitive place. Literacy was low; trade was limited; warfare was endemic. The great centers of wealth were in Asia and the Middle East. China, Japan, Indonesia, India, and Egypt were all prosperous and had developed their own sophisticated technology. Before the Industrial

Revolution, manufacturing meant textile production, luxury good production, and architecture. The urban centers of Asia and the Middle East had textiles, art objects, and architecture that were easily the match of those of Europe. Europe's advantages over these regions came from military conquest and adverse treatment.

Europe had been growing endogenously during the last few centuries of the Middle Ages. However, its big break came from the discovery of the Americas. Mexico and Peru had supplies of silver far in excess of anything available in Europe. The Spanish seizure of the Mayan and Aztec kingdoms provided Europe with a vast supply of silver currency that led to one of the greatest monetary expansions in economic history. This financed both a substantial improvement in European standards of living and a substantial increase in European military power.

Europeans did not always treat their conquered populations well. Consider Java, the economic center of ancient Indonesia. Java is a tropical paradise. It was agriculturally self-sufficient due to its excellent rice lands.

When the Dutch took over Indonesia, they decided to start sugar plantations in Java.

The catch: sugar uses the same ecosystem as rice—wet, coastal marshes. So, the Dutch evicted the Javans from all the good rice lands so that the Dutch could grow sugar. The Javans were forced into highlands, where rice was harder to grow; this led to a general crisis in the food supply.

Worse, the Dutch needed Indonesian labor for the sugar plantations. So they instituted both forced cultivation and taxes that could only be paid in Dutch currency. The only way to earn Dutch currency was to join the Dutch army, work as a servant in a Dutch household, or work on the Dutch sugar plantations. Villages found themselves forced to send workers away from rice paddies where they were needed to work on the sugar plantations to earn their tax money—and the Dutch were also demanding a percentage of the rice crops as well. Rice production per capita languished.

To keep Javans from obtaining currency from commerce or manufacturing as an alternative to plantation work, the Dutch encouraged Chinese in-migration. The Chinese were given preferential access to positions in retail, manufacture, and finance. Javans were kept out. Ethnic inequality was exacerbated, leading to Chinese-Malay hostilities that exist to the present day. Indonesia, once a manufacturing power in its own right, became agricultural, hungry, and poor.

India is a more explicit case of a nation losing its manufacturing capacity because of the self-interest of a colonial power. India's traditional textile center was in Bengal, which had weavers and spinners of distinction. India, however, became a colony of Great Britain. When the Industrial Revolution came, Britain developed factory textiles, which threatened to bankrupt the rest of the world's textile makers. Factory textiles were far cheaper than handmade textiles. British imports could undercut everyone else and dominate the world market for cloth.

Most of the world that was not colonized responded to the British threat by putting tariffs on English textiles. France, the United States, the German States, and the Low Countries all protected their local textile industries with tariffs. This allowed these countries time to catch up with the English technological advantage. Soon all of those nations had their own textile factories and were able to compete in the world clothing market on a level playing field.

India was not able to impose tariffs against the British because it was a colony of the United Kingdom. Britain mandated that India maintain free trade. Cheap British textiles flooded the Indian market. This essentially drove the Bengal weavers out of business. India did not regain a solid manufacturing capacity until after independence.

Readers who are skeptical about the claim that being colonized by a European power leads to underdevelopment should consider the case of Japan. Japan is one of only three nations in Asia that are fully industrialized. The other two, Israel and Singapore, were dirt-poor under colonial rule but became wealthier after independence. Japan is the only Asian member of the G-7. In the 1940s, Japan was able to fight the United States in a major world war, having built all of its own aircraft, battleships, and weaponry. No other nation in Asia had this industrial capacity.

Japan was never colonized by the West.

Not only was Japan never colonized, but in 1633 Japan closed its borders to all foreigners. This not only prevented any economic damage from direct foreign rule but also prevented any threat to Japanese industry from foreign imports as well as any asymmetrical, disadvantageous trade.

Japan is rich. Most of the rest of the Global South is poor.

To be sure, the European colonialists had their good points. They built roads, promoted education, and improved public health.

But someone comparing the history of Japan with that of India or Indonesia may be tempted to say that Japan made the right call. That argument gains force when considered with other disadvantages of economic dealings with the West.

Chapter 22

What Can Go Wrong When Western Companies Invest in Poor Nations

The grievances described in the previous chapter would just be historical trivia if they had no relationship to current circumstances. In the 1700s the British did terrible things to the American economy. However, today the United States and Britain have a collaborative relationship. As a result, Americans do not obsess about the horrible, terrible British. The Fourth of July is just an excuse for picnics and fireworks.

The situation is different for the economic damage the West did to the Global South. The difference is that some of that harm is still being done today. The forms are gentler. Good is mixed in with the bad. But the intelligent African, South Asian, or Latin American observer can still find parallels between the historical record and contemporary economic experience.

Consider the case of multinational corporations. These are companies that are based in one country but have subsidiaries in many other nations of the world. Most of these are American, European, or Japanese—for example, Coca-Cola, General Motors, Toyota. A few of these multinationals are from the Global South, such as Mexico's Cemex.

Multinational corporations investing in poor nations is supposed to be good. The multinational corporations offer to bring in capital and technology. Capital and technology are just what struggling economies need.

With that kind of generous offer, what could go wrong?

The problem is *capital repatriation*. Capital repatriation is when a foreign-owned subsidiary of a multinational corporation transfers its profits out of the local country and into the home country where the multinational's headquarters are located. If the profits of Walmart of Peru are transferred back to the United States, then those profits would produce economic growth and jobs in the United States and not Peru.

How much capital repatriation occurs? This is highly variable depending on the country and the period involved. China makes it difficult to get money out of the country. Singapore lets money leave with few restrictions. In the 1970s, many Latin American governments restricted capital repatriation. In the 1950s, 1960s, and the present day, it has been easy for corporate profits to leave Latin America.

For a good example of what happens when multinational companies "act badly," consider a famous study by Barnet and Muller of the Latin American subsidiaries of American manufacturing companies in the 1960s. They found that the American companies actually started very few new manufacturing operations in Latin America. They instead shopped for preexisting successful companies that had already been built and developed by the local business community. They took operations that already had a substantial income flow and diverted that flow to the United States. The Americans did put in some of their own money and technology to improve local operations. All in all, they found the Americans contributed 43 percent of the financial assets of the company. However, they repatriated 79 percent of the profits to the United States. That represents a substantial drain.

The tendency of Western companies to buy out successful local companies rather than start their own new operations continues to the present day. The Belgian beverage company Ambev entered the Brazilian market by buying out Antarctica and Brahma, the number 1 and 2 beverage brands in Brazil. Walmart built its presence in Brazil by buying out the Bompreco supermarket chain in the northeast and the Sonae chain in the southeast.

Statistically, this produces the odd effect of multinational investment in the Global South being benevolent in the short term (increasing rates of economic growth) and being pernicious in the long term (decreasing rates of economic growth). Foreign direct investment is the technical term for the amount of money invested by businesses in one nation in businesses of another nation. Foreign direct investment is Parsonsian and helpful in the years immediately after purchasing a company. At this point, the American or European company is investing its own funds in improving the operations of the local company—buying new equipment, introducing American technology, and training workers in better procedures. The company is becoming more profitable. It is contributing to local economic growth.

At some point, the American or European owners get the local company to the point at which they want it to be. Thereafter, they stop making investments and upgrades. They start treating the company as a cash cow from which they can withdraw funds to invest in other operations. It is in this later period that the multinational companies become drains on the capital supply of the host nation.

Econometric analyses of both the short-term and the long-term effects of foreign direct investment find that the turnaround point is about five years after the investment. From year zero to year five, foreign direct investment raises rates of economic growth. From year five to year twenty, foreign direct investment lowers rates of economic growth.

Statisticians: note that when there is a positive short-term and a negative long-term effect of foreign direct investment, simple studies that do not break out the time periods get chaotic random overall effects. This is just what you find in the econometric literature. A bunch of studies find positive effects of foreign direct investment, other studies find negative effects, and a lot more find effects only under narrow circumstances.

The East Asians turned against foreign multinationals long before these statistical studies were published. Early on, their governments banned foreign corporations from buying local companies. Japanese companies, such as Honda, Toyota, and Mitsubishi, are all owned by the Japanese. Korean companies, such as Samsung and LG, are all owned by Koreans. China does permit joint ventures between Chinese companies and foreign firms but makes it very hard for profits earned in China to leave the country.

Japan, South Korea, and China have all had three of the highest rates of economic growth in economic history. Countries that permit foreign ownership, such as those in Latin America, have been growing more slowly. Do you think there might be a relationship here?

Chapter 23

CYCLES OF CATASTROPHIC DEBT

One does not need multinational corporations to produce capital repatriation. The most devastating financial drains of the Global South have come from debt crises.

Debt crises occur when poor countries can't make the payments on their loans. Research by Christian Suter and by Carmen Reinhart and Kenneth Rogoff has shown that these crises occur in regular historical cycles. Overconfident banks advance money to countries that are risky prospects. Over time, the questionable loans go sour. The banks get strict about repayment. The repayment plans are so severe they tank the debtor nation's economy. The world goes into financial crisis that can last longer than a decade. Then the world economy recovers. The banks have money to loan. They start another cycle of imperfect lending, setting up the next crisis down the road.

Debt crises are as much the fault of the borrowing nation as the lending nation. The debtor nation is spending more than its means. Some loans are for economic development projects—sensible or misconceived. Some loans are for military purposes—self-defense or pure adventurism. Some loans are for profligate consumption by the elite. Many loans are a mix of everything.

Debt crises poison the relationship between the developed world and the underdeveloped world. It doesn't matter if the poor nations do or do not bear responsibility for their indebtedness. Debt crises and debt repayment plans gut the economy of the less developed nation. Collection efforts are unpopular. How much do you love the bank that took away your grandfather's farm?

There are many stories of how debt crises have produced underdevelopment. One of the most compelling is that of Egypt in the nineteenth century. Of all the nations in the Middle East, Egypt was the most primed to have an industrial revolution. The Nile made Egyptian agriculture highly productive. Egypt's central location made it a nexus of trade between Europe, Asia, and Africa.

In some respects, Egypt resembled the United States. In the early nineteenth century, the United States grew rich by growing cotton in the South, selling it to Great Britain, and using the proceeds to invest in factories in the North. The three great suppliers of cotton to Great Britain were the United States, India, and Egypt. Egypt was quite intentionally following the American model—building its own textile factories with cotton proceeds and investing heavily in railroads and ports. The United States was advantaged over Egypt. The United States had a higher level of education, lower social inequality, and a larger entrepreneurial class. However, Egypt had a countervailing advantage: Egypt's Jumel cotton was the highest-quality, most-sought-after cotton in the world. Egyptian cotton commanded a premium price.

The United States developed. Egypt did not. Debt had a lot to do with this. Egypt got into debt for all of the complicated reasons listed earlier in the chapter. It invested in bona fide development projects, including railroad building, land drainage, and building the Suez Canal. On the other hand, it spent a fortune rebuilding Cairo to make it look European. It fought stupid wars with Turkey and the Sudan. Its leaders enjoyed pharaonic lifestyles.

By the mid-nineteenth century, Egypt was heavily in debt. A substantial part of the problem was that most of Egypt's debt was written in rip-off terms. It was common practice in the nineteenth century for rich nations to disburse to poor nations less than the full value of their loans—claiming the debtor had to pay "fees." The debtor still had to repay the full-face amount of the loan. Egypt's first major bond issue from France was for 28 million francs. Egypt received only 21 million of this.

In 1876, Egypt suspended payment on its loans. The English sent the Royal Navy to Egypt, where it bombarded Alexandria. Egypt had no defense, so it had to capitulate. The financial functions of the Egyptian government were taken over by the English and the French, who ran Egypt for their own advantage. England obtained full formal ownership of the Suez Canal, even though the Egyptians had paid for it, going into debt to do so. The Egyptians still had to repay the Suez construction debt, even though England got 100 percent of the proceeds from the canal. The English and the French gave themselves the proceeds from the Egyptian cotton crop. These were reinvested in England and France rather than Egypt. So, while the United States was reinvesting its cotton profits in industrialization, Egypt could not do that since all the profits remained in Europe. England and France reduced Egypt's government expenditure, which meant limiting Egyptian expenses on education. On the plus side, the Europeans did permit the construction of infrastructure, which Egypt desperately needed. On the minus side, the Europeans prevented the Egyptians from implementing all but the most limited form of tariff protection. Egyptian industry had to deal with competitive pressure from English and French manufactures.

The Egyptian story is not unique. A not dissimilar process occurred in Latin America in the 1980s and 1990s. Latin America got itself into serious debt problems in the 1970s. Some of the money went to development projects. Some of the money went to antipoverty projects. Some of the money was just siphoned off. Venezuela's elite bought more foreign assets in 1981 than the entire value of the loans that were negotiated that year.

When the crunch came, the International Monetary Fund insisted that the Latin American governments shrink their government expenditure in order to pay their debts. Since debts are paid from government revenues, the less money spent on government programs, the more money is available to send to creditors.

This meant that most nations in Latin America reduced their expenditure on public health and hospitals, education, and programs for the poor. Food subsidies, public transportation, and welfare checks shriveled. Many economic development projects were canned. Some of those were no loss. Some were good projects whose loss hurt the economy.

Spending on public security dwindled. This was one of the causes of the rise of narco-gangs in Latin America in the 1990s. If the government is not willing to pay police officers, the drug lords are happy to step in to do the job.

So, poverty increased. Hospitals deteriorated. Education stagnated. Crime soared. And why was all this happening?

To protect the profits of seven rich American banks.

To be sure, there was more to debt repayment than this. Other banks were involved because the loans were syndicated. The world economy depends on a solvent financial system. Etc., etc.

But justifying the impoverishment of nations is not an easy public-relations sell. This would be true even if the case for repayment programs were to be objectively reasonable.

Debt creates hostility between the Global North and the Global South. It did so historically. It does so now.

Chapter 24

East Asian Secrets
of Economic Growth

How do poor countries achieve economic growth in the face of all the obstacles posed by the rich countries? The most successful ones have used a highly advanced form of big government—a strategy known to economists as the *developmentalist state*. This strategy was designed by Japan in the late nineteenth century, perfected by South Korea in the 1960s and 1970s, and brought to a high level of polish by the Chinese today. Japan is the most successful Asian economy; it is the only country in Asia in the G-7, the Council of the World's Largest Industrial Economies. South Korea, during its growth span, achieved the highest rate of growth in economic history. It held that record until China beat it in the 1990s and 2000s. If you were looking to find the secret of economic growth, you would be wise to study Japan, South Korea, and China, all three of which outperformed the United States, Great Britain, and Germany.

How does the developmentalist state work? The key is having a very strong set of government economic planners who tell private companies how they should invest. These countries are not anticapitalist. Companies are privately owned; profits accrue to the owners. But anyone who wants to stay in the good graces of the government follows the official government plan.

For this to work you have to have a very, very competent set of government planners. Japan, Korea, and China all had star teams that could do this. There are wannabe countries that have tried this but did not have the technical skills in the government ministries. If incompetents are running the show, the results are disastrous.

Here is what Japan, Korea, and China actually did:

1. *Restrict firm ownership to Locals. Keep multinational corporations out.* Japan closed its borders from 1633 to 1853. Korea reserved nearly all of its industrial investment for local firms. China was Communist with limited ownership rights for foreign companies. All of the profits are reinvested in their own country rather than being repatriated to the West.
2. *Strictly limit imports for consumption.* Profits were plowed back into investment. All consumption goods are manufactured locally.
3. *Massively invest in education.* Japan in 1870 was the most educated nation in Asia. South Korea was the most educated Asian nation in 1980. China is vigorously trying to catch up.
4. *Develop a long-term plan for the nation to go into the right industries at the right time.* Here is what Korea's plan looked like.

   For most of its history, Korea was extremely poor. Its mountainous terrain led to miserable agriculture. The Korean War destroyed nearly the entire manufacturing capacity of the country. General Park Chung-Hee, the first major planner, knew that Korea had no resources and no money.

   Park's team moved the entire economy into textiles. Most Korean women could sew, and sewing machines were cheap. The poverty of Korea would be a strategic advantage. Low wages would allow Korea to undercut the textile manufacturers in Europe and the United States. Nowadays, we are used to cheap manufacture in Asia. But Park was the first leader to make cheap labor the basis of a development plan. Low wages and long hours allowed Korea to outcompete the textile manufacturers in the rest of the world.

   The second phase of the national plan was to move into electrical appliances. Korea became the leading producer of products such as televisions, stereos, refrigerators, and washing machines. The appliance business required more capital than did textiles, but Korea now had the money to buy equipment. The engineering for these products was relatively simple. Korea's wage advantage became decisive, and Korea came to dominate the world market for appliances.

Now Korea had substantial resources for investment. The next two industries were shipbuilding and steelmaking. These required massive amounts of capital and substantial sophistication in technology. Fortunately, Korea had been using its time during the textile and appliance periods to acquire much of the training it needed. Korean shipbuilding and steelmaking were tremendous successes and Korea became a world leader in these sectors as well.

5. *Induce private firms to cooperate with the national plan by having the government guarantee sales, profits, and cheap credit.* As it happened, the Korean government rarely had to pay up on its profit pledges. Good planning and cheap wages allowed Korean firms to become profitable after relatively short incubation periods.

6. *Prevent Korean firms from going soft by setting strict performance standards in the middle term. Companies that did not hit their targets lost their profit guarantees and the government's goodwill.* In other countries (Brazil and India are good examples), government guarantees can go on and on and on even for companies that are not making measurable progress.

Just because this system worked in East Asia does not mean it will work elsewhere.

If the national plan is not strong, following government instructions will be counterproductive.

If the government is corrupt, industrialists can pay off officials and get their payments and loans without performing.

If the country is politically unstable, the government may have to compromise with industrialists to stay in power. That also means payments and loans without performing.

If the country is weak relative to the United States, it will not be able to keep out American business and will have limited ability to ban foreign imports.

South Korea was a dictatorship, so domestic resistance was not an issue. Korea was critical to American defense interests. If the United States had tried to destabilize South Korea, the North Koreans would have chosen that moment to invade. So Korea could ban American companies with impunity.

South Korea was relatively uncorrupt.

So, South Korea had all the special preconditions necessary for a developmentalist state to be a success.

The Japanese and Chinese cases differ in their details, but the basic stories are much the same.

Big government helped East Asia to develop. Does this have any relevance to the United States?

Chapter 25

Big Government and Prosperity
in the United States

We have seen that the poor countries that have done the best job of catching up economically with the United States have made extensive use of big government. But what about the United States itself? Is big government good or bad for the rich countries?

A lot of Americans are fairly skeptical about the federal government. Some feel the public sector is full of bureaucrats who waste money, interfere with business decisions, and push personal agendas. Others are obsessed with party politics and despise everything from "the other party." Both groups miss a fundamental point.

Big government is essential to the survival of a modern capitalist system. It may not have been needed at the time of Adam Smith. However, technology and societal scale have evolved substantially since Smith's era. Twenty-first-century economies without effective governments die.

What does government do that is actually useful? It provides institutional support for the economy that capitalists cannot provide for themselves. A rational free market does not provide all the goods and services that a society needs, because there are certain legitimate jobs that business won't do.

Business will *not* provide the following services:

1. Defense
2. Education
3. Public health
4. Physical infrastructure (roads, ports, airports)
5. Scientific research

Why won't profit-maximizing investors provide for these fundamental needs? All five items on the list are completely unprofitable. They lose money in the short term.

Can corporations make money from defense? It is highly profitable to sell arms to the government. It is not profitable to fight wars oneself. There is no money to be made sending men and equipment to a battlefield to be destroyed. No major nation uses mercenaries as the primary basis of its armed forces. If there is to be defense, the government must provide armed forces itself.

Education is not profitable. There *is* money to be made educating the children of the rich. Private schools have long existed for society's elite. These institutions offer impressive educations—at even more impressive prices. However, an economy needs *all* its workers to be trained. The poor have to be able to read instructions and do math. There is no money to be made in running schools for slum dwellers. Their parents cannot pay tuition. If there is to be education, the government will have to pay for it.

The same applies to public health. Neither the economy nor the nation will prosper if everyone is dying. The rich can afford antibiotics and can put sewers in their houses. The poor may not be able to afford antibiotics and cannot afford to build sewerage for their rental homes. Untreated sewage creates germs in rich neighborhoods and poor neighborhoods alike. If the rich do not want to catch diseases, the government will have to pay for antibiotics and sewerage for everyone.

Government is also needed to provide infrastructure. An economy cannot survive without adequate roads, airports, and ports. Infrastructure is expensive to build.

To construct a road, one must first acquire vast amounts of land. In the case of urban highways, the land is prime downtown property with a lot of improvements on it. Once the land is acquired, the builder will need vast amounts of concrete and steel cable, along with fleets of large specialized equipment to put this into place. Bridges must be built; tunnels must be excavated; hills may have to be partially removed.

If a capitalist pays for this, what revenue does he or she receive? Just tolls, nothing else. Most of the toll roads in the United States are currently operating at a deficit. The construction costs on projects this large are so high that profitability is wiped out for the first few decades of operation.

Airports are equally expensive. A vast amount of real estate has to be purchased—often from landowners charging premium prices. A large amount of concrete has to be poured. Specialized machinery such as baggage conveyors or radar installations has to be purchased.

What are the revenues from a working airport? Airports can charge landing fees, but these are generally low. The airports sell the airlines gas. They can charge parking fees at the garage. They can charge hotels and restaurants concession fees for the right to locate on the property. Essentially an airport is a convenience store that sells gas and food with a little extra money from a hotel. This hardly pays for the enormous initial investments. There are airports in the private sector that are profitable now—*because the government sold the airport while absorbing the costs of the initial construction.* Without the initial construction charges, airports can make money. But no private corporation would voluntarily build an airport from scratch as a profit-making proposition; no major airport in the United States has ever been constructed by a private company out to make a profit.

Scientific research is equally unremunerative. A small number of engineers or scientists can get rich from new discoveries. They start companies to commercialize their endeavors and become millionaires. But these are the winning lottery tickets of science. Most basic science does not produce a commercializable product of any form. Big flashy breakthroughs are the result of generations of earlier work that didn't earn their sponsors a dime. Someone had to do the basic empirical description, develop the methodologies, and lay out theoretical principles. If a nation needs scientific breakthroughs, the government will have to pay for many years of set-up studies.

So this is why the feds, states, and cities are left with the task of defending the nation, educating the nation's children, eliminating public health hazards, building infrastructure, and financing the research on which the nation's technological prowess depends. The big projects devolve on the feds.

No one wants to be defenseless, illiterate, sick, immobile, and dependent on the technology of foreigners. Yet, the people who would like to shrink big government are implicitly asking for this outcome.

Chapter 26

The Miracle of Airports

The previous chapter discussed how expensive airports are, and how reluctant private capital would be to pay for them. However, no hard evidence was given that airports actually produce economic growth. This chapter has the hard evidence. Both statistical and historical data suggest that airports increase economic growth and do so dramatically.

The two main quantitative studies that have been done on the effects of airports on economic development were done by me in Brazil and John Kasarda in the United States.

I contrast the growth rates of pairs of nearly identical Brazilian states when one state received an airport expansion and the clone state did not. I also compared the growth rates of states before and after they received an airport expansion. Both types of tests showed the same result. There was dramatically higher growth in the states receiving airport expansions; the supergrowth only occurred after the airport expansion was completed.

Commercial agriculture and tourism seem to be particularly responsive to enlargements of airport capacity. In Pernambuco, in Northeastern Brazil, the expansion of the local airport in Recife led to the rapid construction of refrigerated warehouses next to the airport. With the refrigerated warehouses in place, nearby farms shifted over from low-margin corn and bean crops to a sophisticated internationally oriented fruit and vegetable export. Using the new airport, they could send high-markup fruits and vegetables to Europe and Asia. Tourism benefited as well. Airports near attractive beaches were often accompanied by the quick construction of new hotels and coastal resorts along with the creation of vacation packages to encourage tourists to visit the new leisure complex.

John Kasarda shows this applies to the United States as well. Kasarda correlates employment growth with the volume of air traffic in and out of American cities. A cynical reader might think, "What a no-duh finding! Of course rich cities have more air traffic! People want to fly into and out of them!" Kasarda has that angle covered. American air traffic flies on the hub-and-spoke system. Some cities, such as Chicago, Dallas–Fort Worth, Atlanta, and Charlotte, are hubs. Other cities, such as Houston, Detroit, and Kansas City, are not. Hub cities are not necessarily bigger than nonhub cities. Houston is bigger than Dallas. Kasarda's data show that hub cities grow more than nonhub cities. What is driving the growth is the presence of easy air access.

Consider the role that Hartsfield Airport has played in the economic development of Atlanta. In the nineteenth century, the two dominant cities in the South were New Orleans and Atlanta. New Orleans was richer and more important than Atlanta because it was at the mouth of the Mississippi River. The port of New Orleans shipped all the agricultural output from Mississippi, Tennessee, Arkansas, and Louisiana, not to mention much of the output of the Midwest. Atlanta was a rail junction, structurally not all that different from Chattanooga. Hartsfield Airport allowed Atlanta to take off. In the 1920s, airplanes needed to refuel frequently. Pan American Airlines needed a refueling stop for its flights from New York to South America. Atlanta had a better airport than Miami, so Pan Am began to refuel there. The airline liked the facilities at Hartsfield so much that it began to route lots of its flights through Atlanta. As business grew in Atlanta, the town authorities realized that Hartsfield was a significant asset. They resolved to make sure that Atlanta would always have one of the largest airports in the country with the newest designs. Noncontiguous terminals connected by an underground subway and underground baggage conveyors was a Hartsfield innovation. That is now standard practice in American airports. Companies located in Atlanta because of the ease of transportation.

Contrast Atlanta with the experience of New Orleans. New Orleans would have had problems expanding its airports due to the marshy terrain and the presence of Lake Pontchartrain. Given that, New Orleans was slow to develop its airport capacity and has always lagged behind Atlanta. New Orleans was the dominant commercial city in the South in 1850. It depends on tourism today.

Work by the Marxist geographer Doreen Massey provides further support for Kasarda's argument. Late twentieth-century Britain was marked by a movement of employment away from traditional manufacturing centers in Northern England (such as Tyneside, Liverpool, Manchester, and Birmingham) and lower Scotland (such as Clydeside) to Southeastern Britain in the area around London. This could not be accounted for by any objective economic advantage of the London area, such as access to population or labor, access to raw material, transportation costs relevant to continental export, or access to an educated labor pool. The key factor was proximity to Heathrow Airport. In the postwar era, there was substantial multinational penetration the British industrial structure, with American firms buying up a large percentage of important UK employers. The American executives wanted easy physical access to their offices and production facilities and did not want to travel extensively once they arrived in Britain from the United States. So they tended to relocate offices and production centers to facilities within easy commuting distance of Heathrow Airport in West London. This created a substantial secondary wave of British-owned firms relocating to Southeastern England in order to be able to service and work with these key American-owned companies—with the end result being the dramatic deindustrialization of Northern England.

Note that it is possible to overdo airport construction, just as it is possible to overdo anything else. Spain went on an airport-building binge in the 2000s. Above and beyond the airports the country already had, forty-eight new airports were constructed. Many of these were less than an hour from each other. Only eleven of the new airports were profitable. Some saw no air traffic at all.

But airports in general spur dramatic rates of economic growth. The private sector won't build these. Building airports is the business of government.

Chapter 27

THE ORIGINS OF NATIONAL TECHNOLOGICAL ADVANTAGE

Big government is also responsible for countries achieving strategic technological advantages.

Strategic technological advantage is the key to gaining from unequal terms of trade. If your country has invented something and controls proprietary technology, your nation has a monopoly and can charge monopoly prices. Other countries have to compete with other vendors to sell their goods and sell at low competitive prices.

But how do countries get technological monopolies? The United States has some of the best science and engineering in the world. Americans like to think this is because Americans are smart. But smart people exist everywhere.

America's scientific and engineering dominance comes from the superiority of its higher education. For much of history, the United States has led the world in the percentage of its population with a college education. For much of history, American universities have done far more research than their counterparts in other nations. This has meant that the American workforce has had higher technological skills than have the workforces of other nations. The research from American universities has made the United States a scientific leader.

Industry does little of America's basic research. There are good business reasons for this. Only a very small number of research projects produce breakthroughs that lead to commercially viable projects. Many basic research projects fail completely. Others generate findings that are strictly of interest to specialists but have no obvious applications. The minor projects lay the foundations for the breakthrough findings. However, most basic research does not produce anything even remotely profitable. So, industry concentrates on the higher-return activity of developing commercial applications of technologies that are already known and tested.

Why has college attendance among Americans been so historically high, and why do American universities do so much research? The federal government has been responsible for much of this.

The United States was the only country to create large public universities with cheap tuition in every state or province in the nation. Congress passed the Morrill Acts of 1862 and 1890, which provided federal land to pay for the expenses of creating public universities. These land grants resulted in the creation of seventy universities, including Texas A&M, Ohio State University, the University of California at Berkeley, and Tuskegee. The United States had more college-educated people than did other nations because there were more colleges and universities for them to attend.

The Hatch Act of 1914 provided federal support for agricultural research to be done at university agricultural research stations. In that period, European governments had similar strategies. Danish agriculture, which was particularly high-tech, had long enjoyed research support from the Danish government. Similar programs existed in Norway for fisheries.

The next step forward for the Americans was the GI Bill. The GI Bill allowed veterans of World War II to attend college for free. The government subsidized tuition, fees, and books and contributed to living expenses. Millions of Americans received college benefits from the GI Bill. College enrollment nearly doubled, making the United States the world leader in the percentage of its population with a college education.

Some of the largesse of the GI Bill was motivated by national gratitude for the sacrifices made by our soldiers and sailors to protect freedom. However, larger strategic considerations were at work as well. The United States had just fought World War II. World War II was won on technological superiority. The United States and Nazi Germany had been racing each other to build an atomic bomb. The United States won by a few months. Imagine what history would have looked like if the Germans had discovered the atomic bomb before we did and the Nazis had dropped atomic bombs on London and Moscow. The United States was going into the Cold War against a Soviet Union that was also a nuclear power. The United States could not afford to let the Russians become the technological superpower of the world.

This is what led to the founding of the National Science Foundation. Vannevar Bush, dean of engineering at MIT (no relation to either the presidential Bushes or the baked bean Bushes), went to Washington with a plan to guarantee the long-term scientific superiority of the United States over Russia. The federal government would provide funding for every kind of basic science imaginable: biology, chemistry, physics, the works. The federal government would also provide funding for every kind of social science imaginable: political science, economics, sociology, psychology. The plan was that not only would the United States have stronger armed forces due to military technology, but it would also have a better economy due to civilian technology and would be better able to solve social problems with the use of social technology. Large research grants would be given to universities so that top minds could create new knowledge in every one of these areas. The Communist system would lose out to the Free World on every conceivable performance criterion imaginable. No other nation had any institution comparable to the National Science Foundation.

Later on, the federal government would invest even further in university research. The National Institutes of Health would be created to support biomedical research. The Defense Department would start funding its own research programs as well.

How successful was the decision to have the federal government fund university scientific research?

Jonathan Cole has written a massive history of American universities called, fittingly, *The Great American University*. This is the source material from which much of this chapter draws. In that book, he lists the major scientific discoveries that came out of university research from World War II to the present day. The list is 150 pages long. That section of the book is mind-boggling.

He then reviews the university systems of France, Germany, China, and Britain. While these systems have their strengths and are catching up with us, they cannot compare with our scientific accomplishments in our juggernaut years.

Science by its nature is expensive.

Being technologically subordinate to another nation is even more expensive.

Chapter 28

The Economic Returns
to Funding Scientific Research

How much does federal funding for scientific research return to the economy?

Here are some useful figures on that topic.

The Bank of Boston did an analysis of the economic impact of scientific research on the local economy. Boston has eight major research universities: Harvard, MIT, Boston University, Boston College, Brandeis, Northeastern, U-Mass Boston, and Tufts.

These eight universities employed fifty-one thousand people and provided indirect employment for thirty-seven thousand, not counting those workers employed by the university hospitals, themselves massive employers.

Every year, thirty-two thousand students graduated from these eight universities, many of whom remained in the local economy.

Each year, the universities produced over 250 patents.

Each year, the universities produced over 280 commercial licenses.

Each year the universities produced roughly forty start-ups.

Altogether, the universities contributed $7.4 billion to the regional economy.

To pay for this, the federal government provided $1.5 billion in research contracts and grants.

This is a 393 percent rate of return on the federal government's investment.

Advocates of shrinking the government say that if we transferred money from the government to the private sector, we would increase the supply of funds available for private investment, and therefore increase the rate of economic growth.

How many private-sector investments can you think of that have a 393 percent rate of return?

The highest rate of return of the S&P 500 in the past thirty years was 38 percent in 1995. Most years it is much lower.

In 2020, you would be hard-pressed to find a good corporate bond with a 5 percent rate of return.

If one wanted to create economic growth, why would one move money from an investment with a 393 percent rate of return to an investment with a 38 or 5 percent rate of return?

I don't know either.

Chapter 29

THE TAX REVOLT

How the Conservative Middle Class
Became the Revolutionary Class of Capitalism

We have seen how essential big government is to economic growth.

However, there is a movement to shrink big government and cut taxes. This is not just a matter of Ronald Reagan, Fox News, or Donald Trump. State shrinking and tax cutting are both global phenomena.

Table 29.1 shows twenty-eight nations that have cut personal tax rates since 2000 and, counting the twenty-two clumped at the bottom, fifty-one that have cut corporate taxes.

Why is this happening? The best analysis comes from a 1970's Marxist: James O'Connor. O'Connor's *Fiscal Crisis of the State* argues that political change in capitalism would come to be dominated by a conservative middle class rather than a leftist working class. Taxes would be the mobilizing issue for this new conservatism. The new Right would win at the ballot box; elected conservative officials really would cut taxes and shrink big government. All of this has certainly come to pass.

He also argues that the tax cuts would produce a fiscal crisis—and that fiscal crisis would ultimately sink the economy. This is more disturbing.

Table 29.1. Countries that have lowered tax rates since 2000

Countries lowering personal taxes	Countries lowering corporate taxes
United States	United States
France	France
Belgium	Belgium
Czech Republic	Germany
Denmark	Japan
Hungary	Canada
Luxembourg	United Kingdom
Mexico	Ireland
Netherlands	Brazil
Norway	Colombia
Poland	Czech Republic
Slovak Republic	Denmark
Slovenia	Ecuador
Sweden	Honduras
Colombia	Hong Kong
Croatia	Indonesia
Egypt	Kuwait
Estonia	Malaysia
Finland	Netherlands
Gibraltar	Norway
Latvia	Panama
Malaysia	Portugal
New Zealand	Russia
Panama	Singapore
Thailand	Slovenia
Vietnam	South Africa
Lesotho	Sweden
Yemen	Switzerland
	Vietnam
	At least twenty-two others

Why was there going to be a middle-class tax rebellion?

The short answer is that most of the taxes under capitalism are paid by two groups: small businesses and rich individuals.

Fortune 500 corporations and large banks pay very few taxes. O'Connor calls this group *monopoly capital*. This is because they are entitled, fully legally, to a wide variety of exemptions that they make full use of. The *New York Times* listed no fewer than eighteen Fortune 500 companies that paid no income tax between 2008 and 2015. They include industrial giants such as General Electric and Duke Energy. There is another subset that shields substantial proportions of their income from taxation by moving money overseas. These companies include Apple, Microsoft, Coca-Cola, and Abbott Laboratories. Internet giants such as Google and Amazon benefit from the low rates of taxation on e-business.

There is nothing immoral or shocking about this. Nearly all taxpayers, including me, make the most of the deductions to which they are legally entitled. Fortune 500 companies are simply entitled to more breaks than the rest of us.

The poor pay very few taxes. They simply don't have any money.

So who picks up the tab? Small businesses and rich individuals. For all the discussion of the unfairness of the "top 1 percent," the top 1 percent actually pays plenty of taxes. When Bill Gates was at Microsoft, his company paid a relatively small share of its income in taxes. Bill Gates in contrast probably paid and still pays a fat share of his income in taxes. What happens to Bill Gates happens to doctors, lawyers, independent accountants, and small business owners. Doctors, lawyers, accountants, and small business owners represent the heart of the Tea Party and the antitax Republicans.

I remember a lawyer in Kentucky who once told me (paraphrasing):

> I essentially work for the government. I produce the value in my company with my legal advice. I pay corporate income tax and limited liability entity tax. I pay withholding tax and social security for my workers. I pay the state sales tax for my supplies and the city property tax for my building. When I get home, I pay federal income tax on my income, sales tax on my purchases and property tax on my residence. Most of my work goes straight to the government.

Naturally, being a lawyer, he presented the facts in the form most favorable to himself. But the point he makes is valid. As a small businessman, he pays a lot of taxes, which he is legally unable to avoid.

Although small businesses and rich individuals pay the lion's share of federal taxes, they get a small percentage of the benefits of government expenditure. Most government procurement goes to large companies. This is particularly the case in defense, where small operators are in no position to build sophisticated large-scale armaments.

Government bailouts are reserved for monopoly capital. Small businesses and individuals are left to go bankrupt. In the most recent financial crisis, the federal government provided millions to protect General Motors and the Wall Street banks. Major employers and Wall Street banks, love them or hate them, are vital for the functioning of the economy. In contrast, the economy will not notably be affected if a beauty parlor or auto body shop goes bankrupt. The government rescues large firms whose failure would cost thousands of people their jobs. Small firms are left to survive on their own.

Government regulations favor large businesses rather than small, because monopoly capital has access to lobbying firms, political contributions, and the voting base of their own employees.

Small businesses, wealthy individuals, and the middle class are paying a disproportionately large amount of the expenses of the government while receiving a disproportionately small amount of government benefits. This makes those taxpayers resentful of government bureaucrats, welfare programs, and government waste.

If government expenditure is generally useless, then these shrink-the-state initiatives would be harmless or even beneficial. However, if government expenditure actually does something useful, then the shrink-the-state movement is intrinsically dangerous. Shrinking America's military reach seems unwise in a world that is increasingly hostile to American interests. Reducing expenses on education seems unwise in a world where economies depend on technological excellence. Reducing expenditure on law enforcement seems unwise in a world with increasing gang violence. Reducing expenditure on ecological preservation seems unwise on a planet with dwindling natural resources and increased environmental threats. Reducing expenditure on public health seems unwise in a world where germs are becoming steadily antibiotic resistant and new diseases are coming into being.

Will all of this lead to economic collapse tomorrow?

No. The economy will still lurch along.

But a nation that cannot defend itself is a nation that has to cede to the policy wishes of foreign powers. Economic and political dominance will shift to those countries that are better financed and that have better technology.

Death from economic stagnation is slow. Flint, Michigan, used to be a wealthy, prosperous city. Now it is a poverty zone with few economic prospects.

Flint is better off than the slums of Lagos, Nigeria. But it is poorer now than it was at midcentury.

I would rather live in Silicon Valley than in Flint. If higher taxes are necessary to create and maintain the societal and scientific infrastructure of Silicon Valley, the taxes would seem to be a relatively fair trade.

Chapter 30

Why Tax Cuts Do Not Create Jobs

There is an obvious counter to the previous argument.

What if cutting taxes creates jobs?

If cutting taxes produced an immediate short-term surge in employment, the resulting economic growth might produce enough revenues to maintain government services. Advocates for tax cuts promise dramatic increases in the number of new jobs, with rising income for all.

Is this really true?

The standard argument for why tax cuts increase GDP is that reducing taxes takes money away from wasteful government bureaucrats. The money is put in the hands of entrepreneurs and investors. More investment equals more growth.

This argument sounds appealing. On closer examination, it falls apart for six different reasons.

1. In a Globalized Economy, Proceeds from American Tax Cuts May Be Invested Overseas

A tax cut in the United States can produce more jobs in China than in the United States. All modern economies are globalized. Corporations have affiliates and subcontracting relationships all over the world. Rational executives will invest any windfalls in whatever nation offers the highest return—not necessarily the United States.

George Bush instituted two major tax cuts, in 2001 and 2003. This should have induced a burst of investment in the United States. However, the Congressional Research Service found that American investment in foreign countries increased dramatically in the period after the tax cut. European firms sent *less* out of their countries than we did! The outflow of American investment dollars did *not* go to tax havens like Singapore. They generally went to Europe, which has high tax rates. So our tax cuts neither attracted foreign money to us nor kept our money in the United States.

2. Firms Do Not Always Lower Employment When Taxes Are High

Economic theory challenges the argument that high taxes reduce employment. The literature on public finance maintains that taxation produces two contradictory effects on investment and employment, one an income effect and the other a substitution effect. The claim that taxation reduces investment involves a *substitution* effect, an argument that lowered profitability induces capitalists to move capital to other investments. This is counteracted somewhat by the *income* effect. In the face of a tax, entrepreneurs with a goal of making a fixed amount of money increase their investments to compensate for lost revenues. It is difficult a priori to specify which of the two types of effects predominates.

Actual studies of firms undergoing tax increases do not show that raising taxes lowers employment. One study found that some American employers reacted to tax increases by raising prices rather than cutting jobs. Other employers simply tolerated lower profit margins. A study of textile firms in Morocco showed that a tax *increase* actually improved the long-term survival of the industry. Firms had been stagnating in a comfort zone using outdated technology. The tax increase was a wake-up call inducing Moroccan companies to upgrade. After the new machinery was acquired, profits and employment levels rose.

3. Tax Breaks and Tax Evasion Reduce the Impact of Cutting Tax Rates

Almost nobody pays the full on-the-books tax rate on their income. Legally, both individuals and companies are entitled to deductions. People take a lot of these. The *Huffington Post* reports a number of major US corporations legally pay no corporate income tax whatsoever. In poorer countries, companies solve the tax problem simply by not paying their taxes. Tax evasion is widespread in southern Europe, Latin America, sub-Saharan Africa, and much of Asia. Whether legally or illegally, if companies are avoiding taxes, cutting the rates won't have much of an effect on corporate profits.

4. Most Business Failures Are Caused by Something Other Than Taxation

High taxes don't drive firms out of business. There is a literature studying the cause of corporate bankruptcies and firm closings. The methodology is simple: when a firm closes, you ask the owner what caused the firm to die. The two most common causes of corporate death are insufficient sales and inability to get credit. Taxes are mentioned as being a problem in very few cases.

5. Taxes Are Not the Biggest Determinant of Corporate Success

Taxes are actually a fairly minor component of total costs. The two biggest expenses that companies face are raw materials and labor. It is far more important to obtain cuts in the prices paid to vendors or the salaries paid to workers than it is to reduce taxes. When companies move to China, they do not do so to get breaks on taxes. They are trying to obtain cheap Chinese labor.

Sometimes, what matters for corporate survival is not overall costs but getting the critical inputs the company needs. California's taxes are high. But if a software company wants the best programming talent, it had better locate in Silicon Valley. A theater company can pay fewer taxes if it locates in Oklahoma. But if the company wants a big Broadway hit, New York is where it has to be. Raising taxes is not going to drive software companies out of California or theater companies out of New York. Paying fewer taxes will be less important than developing must-have software or creating a blockbuster show.

6. The Data Do Not Show Any Relationship between Taxes and Job Growth

One-third of the studies show no effect of tax rates on job growth. One-third of the studies support the tax-cut argument by showing tax cuts leading to job growth. One-third of the studies show exactly the opposite: tax cuts leading to greater unemployment. Negative studies outnumber the positive ones two to one.

Logic does not support the argument that lowering taxes produces jobs. There is no consistent statistical evidence that lowering taxes produces jobs. But cutting taxes does undercut national defense, infrastructure, science, education, crime prevention, and with it, long-term investment in economic growth.

The benefits of tax cuts are ephemeral or fictive. The damage from tax cuts is both lasting and substantive.

Chapter 31

THE EXPLOSION OF CRIME
IN THE GLOBAL SOUTH

Crime has steadily declined in the wealthy industrialized nations. This is not at all the case in the rest of the world. Crime statistics are poor in most of the underdeveloped world, making it difficult to make inferences about trends and exact numbers. However, there is no question that absolute levels of violent crime are quite high. The World Population Review provides the statistics shown in table 31.1 about global homicide rates.

This table intentionally reports statistics from the most crime-prone of the populous poor nations. Those rates are four to sixteen times higher than the rate in the United States. A typical quieter place is the Philippines, which reports a homicide rate of eleven. That figure probably reflects higher homicide rates in Manila and lower rates in rural villages. That said, the Philippines are still twice as violent as the United States.

Kidnappings are an even greater concern than homicide. Kidnapping statistics are completely unreliable. The families of most victims do not report the incident for fear of having the victim killed. In 2019, the US State

Department identified thirty-five countries as having high risks of kidnapping (see table 31.2).

Note that this is a list of countries where the State Department considers Americans to be in danger from kidnapping. There are many countries where kidnapping is common but confined to locals with little risk to Americans.

Kidnapping is a particularly severe problem in Mexico; 2013 was a particularly bad year, in which 1700 people were kidnapped. Kidnappings dropped to about 1200 a year, but they have continued at that level fairly consistently.

Table 31.1. Homicide rates by country, 2020 (estimated)

Country	Homicide rate (per 100K population)
El Salvador	83
Honduras	56
Jamaica	47
South Africa	34
Brazil	30
Guatemala	27
Colombia	25
Central African Republic	20
Mexico	19
United States	5

Table 31.2. Countries identified by the US State Department as having high kidnapping risks in 2019

Afghanistan	Iraq	Russian Federation
Algeria	Kenya	Somalia
Angola	Lebanon	South Sudan
Bangladesh	Libya	Sudan
Burkina Faso	Malaysia	Syria
Cameroon	Mali	Trinidad and Tobago
Central African Republic	Mexico	Turkey
Colombia	Niger	Uganda
Dem. Rep. of Congo	Nigeria	Ukraine
Ethiopia	Pakistan	Venezuela
Haiti	Papua New Guinea	Yemen
Iran	Philippines	

Table 31.3. Ten famous Brazilian kidnappings

Patricia Abranavel	2001	Daughter of TV celebrity. $250,000 ransom.
Wellington Comargo	1998	Gospel singer. $300,000 ransom. Victim lost an ear due to slow pay.
Aperecida Schunck	2016	Mother-in-law of auto racing magnate. Rescued.
Edevair de Souza Faria	1994	Father of soccer player. Rescued.
Abilio Diniz	1989	Owner of large supermarket chain. Rescued.
Washington Olivetto	2002	Ad executive. Rescued.
Eloa Pimentel	2008	15 Year Old Girl. Killed.
Liana Friedenbach and Felipe Caffé	2003	Students. Killed.
Bus #174	2000	Entire bus taken hostage. One hostage died.
Bus on Rio Niteroi Bridge	2019	Entire bus taken hostage. Rescued.

Brazil has a long history of kidnapping (see table 31.3). Just in the state of Pernambuco alone, a not especially violent state, there were 171 kidnappings in 2017. In the city of São Paulo, a more violent place, there were 129 cases of kidnapping in the first four months of 2017. In the 1990s, kidnappings were generally limited to very wealthy victims; the ransoms were astronomical. Over time, the kidnappers became more and more sophisticated and learned how much could be obtained for kidnapping victims who were middle class or semiwealthy. Celebrity victims have the advantage of being able to publicize their plights and have police organize rescues. Less-well-known victims often have to pay. Bus kidnappings are rare; the assailants in the two cases shown in the table were probably mentally ill. The Eloa Pimentel case was domestic violence. The other cases involved career criminals operating with a profit motive. Everyday kidnappings tend to be small scale. Common ransoms involve the amount of money that can be withdrawn from a few visits to an ATM.

It would be an understatement to say that criminal gangs have been out of control in Brazil. Here is an extreme story from 2002 that I experienced indirectly. A day before I arrived in Rio de Janeiro, the entire city had been shut down by a gang. Cars with sound systems drove through the rich neighborhoods of Copacabana, Ipanema, and Leblon and the financial center of the city ordering all businesses and offices to close immediately or face punishment. Fifteen minutes later, businesses that did not close received a telephone call with a stronger order to close. Those that had still not closed got another call with explicit threats. No businesses remained open after the second call. This particular shutdown had been ordered by a particularly flashy gang, the Comando Vermelho (Red Command), somewhat on a whim by their leader.

Other acts of gang violence have been more purposive. That same year, the army and elite police forces had invaded two slum neighborhoods looking for the killer of Tim Lopes. Tim Lopes was a reporter for TV Globo who had been surreptitiously filming a gang party in the slums while working on a story about child prostitution. The gang members caught him in the act, gave him a summary trial, and then tortured him to death. The police flooded the slums looking for the killers. The gangs did not like the massive police presence on their home turf. So early one morning, before the stores were open, a bomb was tossed from a car into the front of Shopping Rio Sul, the biggest shopping mall in the city. The bomb was a diversionary tactic. While the police were investigating the attack on the mall, other cars drove to the Rio de Janeiro city hall and machine-gunned all the offices on the lowest three floors. The attack occurred before anyone had come to work; the bullets left broken windows and holes in drywall. But the gangs had made clear what they had the potential of doing.

Soon afterward, the government announced a new "beach safety" initiative by which police would be assigned to the beaches to protect foreign tourists. This reassignment of police essentially pulled the police out of the slums, allowing the gang members to go back to their normal activities. Later on, some people would be arrested for the Tim Lopes murder. However, the gangs that committed the crime were able to continue their activities without interruption.

Are criminal gangs powerful in Brazil? Yes.

The language used to describe gangs is "O Poder Paralelo" (the Parallel Power).

What allowed criminals to become the Parallel Power?

Chapter 32

The Parallel Power

The Criminal Second State

Why are gangs so powerful in Latin America?

1. Latin America is poor.
2. Gangs get politicians elected and keep them in power. This makes the government an implicit ally of the criminals.
3. Gangs provide social services to poor people that the government can't or won't. This allows some gang leaders to play Robin Hood and become popular.
4. Some of the criminals have full legal impunity. This is especially the case when the gang leaders/members are either politicians or cops.

Poverty. The poverty factor is pretty obvious. Countries with low GDPs have lots of crime. When opportunities for legitimate employment are scarce or unremunerative, people turn to crime because crime pays. Latin America is poor.

Gangs get politicians elected. Democracy can unleash organized crime. Crime rates were low in Brazil when it was a dictatorship. The generals ran the country and that was that. When the military abdicated and called elections, the new candidates had little experience in running for office. Candidates made deals with anyone who would offer them assistance. In Rio de Janeiro, this meant allying with the *bicheiros*, small-time criminals who ran neighborhood lotteries. Rio de Janeiro became very competitive electorally, with control of the city seesawing between left and right. The criminal alliances continued to be essential. Over time, drug lords replaced the *bicheiros*. (Cocaine is more lucrative than five-dollar lotteries.) Because different neighborhoods were controlled by different gangs, most politicians could find some drug lord with whom to ally.

Gangsters are good at stuffing ballot boxes. They induce local officials to change counts. They tell people who to vote for. If guys with guns tell you who to vote for, it is probably best to do as they say. However, there are many neighborhoods where the gang leader's opinion is genuinely trusted. The drug lord may have set up a deal with the candidate. The neighborhood may get benefits, like a new sewer, if the residents vote the right way.

Often a real grievance among the slum dwellers is harassment by the police. Police can be racist, hassle local kids, and shake down local residents for bribes. Having the local gangster make a political arrangement that gets the police to back off the neighborhood is a good deal for everybody.

Gangs provide public services when the government fails to do so. Public services in poor neighborhoods are terrible. Infrastructure is nonexistent or not maintained. Schools are not good. Hospitals are overcrowded and low quality. Assistance in a life crisis can be hard to get.

Churches and philanthropists help fill the gap. They run charities, build schools and clinics, and take care of the needs of parishioners and clients. Gangs don't build schools but they do their part.

Have a baby in pain and you're facing an eight-hour wait at the hospital? A few guys with submachine guns can get you in right away.

Your store about to close? You might get a loan on very soft terms. You might even get a gift. Hey, you're a nice person—and you're loyal.

Someone stalking and threatening your daughter? The police won't do a thing? There are guys on the street who can find and discipline the creep.

Furthermore, the parties thrown by Brazilian drug lords, which are open to the neighborhood, are legendary. The food and music are incredible. Any recreational substance you want will be available. The late-night doings will be wild. You won't get that kind of entertainment from a charity or a church. The concert sponsored by the Ministry of Culture can't compare.

Impunity. One of the simplest ways for organized crime to take over a country is for there to be no legal punishment of criminal activity.

In Brazil, getting legal immunity is simple. The constitution specifies that no politician holding elected office may be arrested or criminally charged. This was put in after the military dictatorship, to prevent the detention and torture of political opponents.

But the system has been abused. Gang leaders who are in legal trouble can run for alderman or state representative. Winning elections is simple given gang control of whole neighborhoods. Once the gang leader is in office, he is untouchable.

Immunity can also come from buying off members of the police force, the district attorney's office, or the judiciary.

Immunity can also come from details of legal procedure. In Brazil, most cases of police misbehavior are investigated only by the police themselves. Cover-ups are the rule rather than the exception.

There is a special form of immunity associated with the "militias." Militias are paramilitary gangs and death squads run by former or present-day police officers working both sides of the law. They often run their own rackets for personal gain. One documented practice is playing "catch and release" with drug lords. Militias arrest gang leaders under the working assumption that the gangs will pay for their release. In these cases, drug arrests are no more than temporary kidnappings. Another tactic is using arrests to clear out other gangs' territories so the militia can seize the drug business for itself.

The militias can count not only on the tacit support of other police and judges but also on the patronage of politicians at high levels. The current president of Brazil, Jair Bolsonaro, a retired military officer, is well known to have extensive ties to militias in both Rio de Janeiro and São Paulo. Militias in both cities worked to get him elected.

Not all paramilitary groups are criminal. Some are simple vigilante organizations—conservative, violent, but not out for themselves. But in Brazil, many of the militias have crossed the criminal line; they are both dangerous and de facto immune from prosecution.

Note these stories have an extra element. Both the gangs and the militias persist because of high levels of corruption. Corruption completely undercuts state effectiveness. Why is there so much corruption in the Global South?

Chapter 33

A Guide to Corruption
for Naive Idealists

When governments are corrupt, nothing works. Maintaining the integrity of government is integral to societal functioning. But what causes governments to become corrupt?

It is not a matter of simple morality. It is not the case that evil people take bribes and good people do not take bribes. Nor is it the case that ethical standards are high in the United States and Europe, and low in the rest of the world.

A good way for Americans to alienate themselves from the rest of the world is to make public pronouncements that the Ukraine is corrupt or that Puerto Rico is corrupt and that such places should not be engaged with until they clean up their acts. Such pieties ring hollow for the following reasons:

1. When Americans or other foreigners go to these other countries, they often engage in behaviors as corrupt as or more corrupt than the behaviors of locals. Residents of corrupt nations know what

schemes, scams, and payoffs look like. They know who is doing what with whom, where the money is going, and what the money is supposed to buy. Americans and Europeans may act with transparency and procedural correctness in their home countries. Ethical standards slip when business is being done in a country where "corruption is normal here, right?"

2. Corruption is usually carefully framed in a manner so as to protect the moral integrity and reputation of both payer and payee. There is as much social sophistication and nuance in the paying of a bribe as there is in the making of a sexual proposition. Of course, people make suggestions of side payments, just as people make suggestions of further nocturnal entertainment. But it is generally insulting and crude to offer payment baldly in an explicit quid pro quo. The response of most officials offered a naked payment will be "Who the hell do you think I am?" Expect froideur and outright hostility from that point onward.

Every country has its own rituals and its own style of handling informal payments. One method is to invoke chivalry and the need for the strong to protect the weak. A person with a problem goes to a powerful person who could possibly understand the gravity of the situation. The protector, out of the goodness of his heart, helps another human being. The rules were impersonal and savage; they were going to hurt a decent human being for no reason. The person who was protected is profoundly grateful for that protection and offers a thank-you present to acknowledge the efforts taken on their behalf and to show respect for someone with the decency to protect human beings in need.

Note that this kind of transfer works best within the context of a long-term relationship. The underling has a friend in high places whom he or she could turn to when faced with a serious problem. The official involved takes care of good people who deserve to be taken care of. The money is simply a matter of respect and gratitude.

Often these exchanges can represent a fundamental alliance and relationship of long-term mutual assistance. The underling works to see that his or her patron gets reelected and is comfortable. The underling makes donations to see that his or her patron gets reelected and is comfortable. The patron would absolutely take care of the underling's comfort and well-being—even if no cash was involved in the particular matter that must be seen to on a given day.

Often corruption occurs while maintaining all outward appearances of complete professionalism. An administrator needs to transfer public money to private hands—either those of his allies or those of his proxies. He is supervising a major construction project that may require consultants. The fees for those consultants could be very high. Those consultants for purely technical reasons may suggest a set of project specifications that could be met by only one particular private vendor. Naturally, because that vendor has unique capacities, the fees for that vendor's services could be very high. A large percentage of the budget has been diverted to special interests; yet technically, everything is completely proper.

Bribery requires skill and sophistication. One has to know the rules of the game. Maria Zaloznaya, a sociologist who has studied corruption in Russia and the Ukraine, shows that corruption is most likely to occur among people who have been specifically trained in bribery. They need to know who to talk to and how things are done.

Some of the rules are designed to prevent detection. One might not hand over large amounts of cash at a public meeting. (This is not a universal rule. In Japan, politicians have been known to come to the weddings of key supporters and conspicuously leave bundles of bills as a wedding gift.)

However, some of the rituals are designed to protect the moral integrity and self-worth of the participants. They are a part of a social construction to show that what is transpiring is virtuous. Heroic public leaders protect the most vulnerable members of their constituencies by thwarting the operation of irrational, impersonal laws that crush innocents who cannot protect themselves. The politician can congratulate himself on his great personal decency, as he floats in the swimming pool of his swag-paid-for condominium in Key Biscayne.

If you are in a country where you have not been taught the proper way to bribe, don't do it! A truly predatory police officer or official will take advantage of your willingness to pay money to milk you for everything you've got.

If you want to understand why some countries are corrupt while others are transparent, don't look at good and evil, or some fundamental lack of ethics or professionalism. The people who take bribes are often good people. The question is, What circumstances drive good people to sell out?

Chapter 34

TECHNICAL DEMORALIZATION

Why are officials in poor countries more likely to be corrupt than officials in rich countries? One reason is that even if these officials played things straight, they simply lack the resources to do their jobs. The condition of being unable to do your job through no fault of your own can be called *technical demoralization*.

In rich countries, such as Denmark, social problems are relatively modest. Much of the population has enough money to solve their own problems themselves. Crime rates are low. People are generally healthy. The size of the poverty population is small. The size of government budgets is large. So, government officials have small, relatively tractable social issues they are expected to deal with. They have substantial amounts of money and personnel in their departments with which to confront those social issues.

In a poor country such as Cambodia, the population with needs is massive. Individuals do not have enough money to solve their problems themselves. Crime rates are high. Disease and sickness are widespread. The size of the poverty population is massive. Likewise, since the country is poor, the government is poor. So, government budgets are relatively small. In an underdeveloped nation, government officials have massive intractable social issues they are expected to deal with and almost no money to apply to the task. Technical demoralization is widespread.

When trying to do your job is a joke, it no longer really matters whether you follow norms of professionalism or not. All of those wonderful dreams you had in graduate school or professional school count for nothing. Nothing gets done. Nothing is ever going to get done. There is no reason not to take care of your family and earn a little money on the side. If a little money turns into a lot of money, well, at least you are turning out to be good at something.

If the public official is in law enforcement, technical demoralization is relevant only to his inability to make a contribution to fighting crime. The officer may not even be capable of protecting himself or his family. Think about the work of a police officer in a country with a lot of drug traffic. The salary of a police officer in Latin America or Afghanistan is generally modest. The officer often has to live in the same working-class neighborhoods that are effectively under the control of the drug lords. One police officer is not going to be able to take out a cartel. The drug lord knows where the officer lives. He knows where the officer's parents live. He knows how to find the children of the officer's brothers and sisters. Even if the cop is completely courageous and is willing (in the style of a Hollywood movie) to take on a personal assault against himself, he cannot protect everyone in his family. So when the drug lord's men come over, nice and friendly, and offer to help the cop out financially, the officer would be hard-pressed to refuse the offer.

This leads to a sickening feedback cycle.
Inability to reduce crime causes police corruption.
and
Police corruption makes it even harder to reduce crime.
The two processes reinforce each other.

The same thing can occur in any branch of government. Public health officials who will never be able to lower the amount of disease in their districts sign off on big, white elephant hospital projects where they can get generous side fees for "consulting." Engineers who will never be able to build enough roads to accommodate the traffic needs of overpopulated cities throw their projects to shabby, politically connected contractors who stint on materials. Game wardens who are expected to patrol hundreds of square miles against bands of armed men looking for ivory or rare animals will be just as happy to take seventy-five dollars to conveniently disappear. In the jungle, it could be a long time before anyone finds that game warden's body.

Corruption is completely demoralizing—even if it is caused by technical demoralization. Can anything be done to clean up governments that have become completely and totally dirty?

Chapter 35

What It Takes to Clean Up Corruption

The world wants to see corruption cleaned up. Historically, this has been done, but it is very difficult.

There are four methods for cleaning up bureaucracy. I rank them from worst to best.

1. Cutting off funds to the offices of corrupt bureaucrats. Makes the officeholders you have left much worse.
2. The old Max Weber solution of imposing formal rational-technical bureaucracy. It is very easy to undercut.
3. Creating brand-new departments of young, idealistic uncorrupted officials. Stellar results today. No promises for the long-term.
4. Civil service reform, which applies the Max Weber solution to every office in the government. Requires massive economic growth.

Defunding Corrupt Offices

There is nothing more emotionally satisfying than cutting off funds to corrupt offices. Taxpayers don't want to pay money to governments where all the money disappears down a rat hole.

The trouble is that the rats have first access to the trough.

When money is disappearing, the rats line their own pockets first. This leaves a smaller remainder for actually doing the work of the agency. Technical demoralization gets worse. If the honest functionaries could not do anything with the old budget, they will be able to do even less with the new budget. Behavior gets worse rather than better.

Imposing Weberian Formal Rational Bureaucracy

Readers who have taken introductory sociology may remember Max Weber and Weberian bureaucracy. *Bureaucracy* in the Weberian sense refers to super-rational, hyperefficient administration. Weber argued that it is the dominant form of organization in the world today. Administrators follow the rules, do what they are supposed to do, and are penalized if they fail to do so. An official takes a bribe? He or she is punished so the offense never happens again.

The four pillars of Weberian bureaucracy are as follows:

1. *Hierarchy* so everyone knows unambiguously who their boss is.
2. *Written rules* so there are no excuses for not knowing what you are supposed to do.
3. *Written record keeping* so we can trace all employee violations and punish them.
4. *Recruitment, promotion, and reward exclusively on merit.* Follow the rules and be rewarded. Break the rules and feel economic pain.

Why does bureaucracy fail to stop corruption in so many countries? Because organizations are neither rewarded for "doing their jobs" nor punished for "not doing their jobs." If the school district is used to make jobs for political supporters of the current regime, then whether employees actually teach children doesn't matter. If the police department will survive regardless of whether it catches crooks, then there is little motivation to actually catch crooks.

If organizations are not rewarded for doing their official jobs, the people within these organizations will not bother to do their official jobs.

Create New Superstar Departments to Accomplish What Old Corrupt Departments Won't

In Brazil, elected politicians need to give away lots of public jobs to reward their supporters. However, they also need accomplishments to justify their future reelection.

Their solution is an old Brazilian trick described by Barbara Geddings. Take preexisting government departments and cram them full of political appointees. Then create a brand-new department designed to solve the problem on which the politician campaigned. Give it a big budget and hire idealistic superstars to staff the new team. Require it to achieve dramatic results by the next election. Make sure no obstacles stand in its way.

These Brazilian superstar departments achieve dramatic success. However, the limits of this system become apparent with each new election. Every new administration has to find new public jobs for the supporters of the most recent campaign. This has to be achieved by larding up the old department that was the last administration's superstar. Then to create its own accomplishments, the administration starts its own brand-new superstar department.

This process can't go on forever. Run long enough, you get a few good departments and a gigantic burden of deadweight.

The Permanent Enduring Fix: Civil Service Reform

Civil service reform means undertaking a Weberian cleanup of the entire governmental structure. All public jobs require top scores on civil service exams. Public servants earn no income outside of their official salaries.

This can work. However, it requires a society that has no further interest in bribery. There are two situations where this has occurred: the Trevelyan

Act in Britain in 1870, and the cleanup of public governance in Singapore in the 1960s and 1970s.

The Trevelyan Act ended patronage appointment in the United Kingdom permanently. At that time, Britain was one of the wealthiest nations in the world—and had been for two hundred years. There were far more lucrative ways to make money than holding a government job. Patronage jobs were not attractive. The business community wanted clean, efficient government. There was no reason for them not to get it.

Corruption was cleaned up in Singapore in the 1960s and 1970s. When the first anticorruption act was passed in 1959, the conditions for reform in Singapore were shaky. The country was poor and in political flux relative to potential control by Malaya. After Singapore was definitively made independent, the economy began to grow explosively. Singapore was soon to be the richest nation in Southeast Asia. Dramatic economic growth undercut the attractiveness and importance of patronage jobs.

Furthermore, Prime Minister Lee Kuan Yew was in the middle of forty-five years of unbroken power. He was strong enough not to need patronage to keep himself in office. Dramatic economic growth and iron-clad political power made complete civil service reform possible.

What would it take for other countries to follow in Britain's or Singapore's footsteps?

A rock-solid economy.

Having a leader in rock-solid control doesn't hurt.

How many poor countries have solid-enough economic growth and government to be able to successfully implement civil service reform?

I would say that number is very small.

Chapter 36

Ethnic Violence

The Economic Basis of Hatred

Corruption may be bad. But it does not lead to mass violence.

Ethnic hatred. That leads to mass violence.

Ethnic hatred is not some fundamental human universal.

It is not the case that all Hindus hate Muslims or that all Muslims hate Hindus or all Hutus hate Tutsis or all Germans hate Jews.

It is not the case that the massacre that took place in 1723 or 1904 or whenever burns in the hearts of all descendants of the victims eternally or that someday, somehow, revenge is going to be inevitable.

It is not even the case that the descendants will necessarily think of themselves as Hindu or Muslim or Tutsi or German.

Ethnic identity is something that is turned on and off. People invoke whatever ethnicity they are entitled to, to the degree that it is advantageous at the moment. I come from Boston and went to school on the East Coast. I have lived in Texas for thirty years. I can be as East Coast as I want to be. I can be as Texan as I want to be. I am a Jewish person who converted to Buddhism. I can be as Jewish as I want to be. I can be as Buddhist as I want to be.

Sometimes one's ethnic identity is forced upon one by others. I have not been served in a restaurant because the owner thought I was "Israeli." (This did not happen in the United States.) I was not planning on being Jewish that afternoon, but suddenly I was.

So, when orators are telling everyone about the horrible, terrible events of a century ago, and everyone is discussing everything that is wrong with Group X, this is not because they think about these things all the time. They are raising those issues now for a reason.

Ethnic conflicts have an economic base. They are fought over money. Different nations and different historical periods have different economic issues at stake. The form of ethnic conflicts is very local specific. Here are some of the most common forms:

1. *Hostility to a middle-class minority in a peripheral agrarian nation.* Sociologists call this ethnic formation a *middleman minority*. This occurs in a situation where some sort of overlord is trying to keep the population working in the fields to produce export crops. In Eastern Europe, local nobles imposed serfdom on their own populations so that local grains could be grown with coerced labor. In Indonesia, the Dutch banned the local Malay majority from working in manufacture or commerce. This was done to force them to work instead on the Dutch East Indies Company's sugar plantations.

    In both settings, it was impossible to have everyone working on the fields as coerced labor because some manufacture had to be done, and there was the need for some retail and some banking. To meet this need, ethnic minorities were recruited to fill these roles. The Dutch imported Chinese merchants to serve the retail function in Indonesia. Eastern European elites did their banking with Jews.

    Following this logic, Jews and Chinese became educated since they needed to be literate to pursue their trades. The local Poles, Ukrainians, and Malays were kept uneducated. This led to the expected conflicts between educated and uneducated people, as the

Jews and Chinese viewed the locals as ignorant peasants, while the locals viewed the Jews and Chinese as effete snobs.

Credit relations also led to conflict. Peasants had to borrow from moneylenders to buy their annual seeds and supplies. When crops failed, there would be the obvious disputes between borrows and lenders.

Purging minorities instantly solved debt problems. Purges were also a powerful response to snobbery and disrespect.

Purges happened often.

2. *Cheap labor minorities in industrial societies.* This refers to the African American situation in the present-day United States—and the Afro-X situation in Canada and Europe. It also applies to Eastern European minorities in Western Europe. Blacks may have been brought to the Western Hemisphere originally to work as slave labor. But with the plantation economy dead and much of American agriculture mechanized, blacks now largely serve as a source of cheap labor. The economic conflicts are typically between fractions of the working class competing over ever-decreasing supplies of manual and blue-collar jobs.

3. *Anti-immigration hostilities in industrial societies.* See previous paragraph.

4. *Conflict over the control of a corrupt state.* Corrupt states do not give benefits to everyone regardless of merit. Benefits are concentrated among those who are essential to keeping the elite in power. In many countries, the regime provides government services exclusively to its own ethnic group. If the other ethnic group were to ever obtain power, the first group would move from receiving all the benefits to receiving none. If the first group wants schooling, roads, or jobs, it had better support the current regime. This certainly characterizes Sunni-Shia conflicts in Iraq. Hutu-Tutsi conflict in Rwanda had this form as well, except in that case, there were conflicts between Hutus as well. Hausa-Yoruba-Ibo conflicts in Nigeria were almost certainly centered on control of the state and control of the petroleum revenues pertaining to the Nigerian state.

5. *Justification for land seizure.* We forget that one of the most long-term and enduring conflicts has been between peoples of European extraction and indigenous people in the rest of the world. Nearly all

of those conflicts were about land use. Settlers wanted new spaces for farming or ranching. Dispossession was okay because Indians were "savages" and "barbarians."

The arguments made here are tawdry and obvious. I am sure that every reader of this chapter has previously thought of these.

But we forget these obvious economic factors when we discuss cases of ethnic violence. We get caught up in cultural differences, historical grievances, and the content of religions.

Sometimes violence is all about the money, even if the instigators are giving fiery speeches on other topics.

Chapter 37

WORKING AT CREATING
A CULTURE OF HATRED

Most ethnic conflicts have an economic base. But this does not mean prejudice and ethnic hatred play no role. Economics can motivate people to foment a culture of hatred. Once enough people have been socialized into the culture of hatred, it is harder to change behavior and get people to cooperate and trust again.

The Canadian sociologist Matthew Lange has found that ethnic supremacist education is a fundamental source of division in some of the most ethnically divided countries in the world. Supremacist schools are a direct cause of the hostility between Jews and Palestinians in Israel, between Sinhalese and Tamils in Sri Lanka, between Greeks and Turks in Cyprus, between French Quebecois and English Canadians in Quebec, and between hostile ethnic groups in many other nations.

The places Lange writes about are dissimilar, but the causes of xenophobic education generally are the same:

1. Start with a society with two ethnic groups.
2. Give that society a really lame economy.
3. Add a highly educated population in one or both of the ethnic groups.
4. Have unemployment rates be high enough that the highly educated population has a lot of people without jobs.
5. Have some of the highly educated unemployed start schools because they have no other way to make a living.
6. Have those teachers be filled with anger and resentment because of their marginalization, their low income, and their low status.
7. Give those teachers an inflated idea of the profound worth of what they learned in school that gave them those educational credentials.
8. Have those teachers have profound contempt for anyone else who did not learn what they themselves learned in school.
9. If teachers were trained in Sinhalese schools, then only people who know Sinhalese culture are any good. If teachers were trained in Greek schools, then only people who know Hellenic culture are any good. If teachers were trained in French schools, . . . You get the idea.
10. To back up the previous point, they think of lots and lots of reasons why the culture of the other group is pathological and decadent. They have articulate arguments about everything that is wrong with Tamil culture, Turkish culture, and so on.
11. Give them the hope that if they can sell this idea of the superiority of Sinhalese or Greek culture, then they can get laws passed guaranteeing that only those people trained in the proper skills and culture can get government jobs or any kind of superior job at all.
12. Make getting the lock on all good jobs forever such an attractive dream that they start organizing social movements to promote their own culture in the society at large.
13. Have them start organizing political parties, holding rallies, and working with lawyers to write the relevant laws.
14. Have public schools be low quality or unavailable, so that lots of children end up in the private schools where these people teach.
15. Have some of these zealots end up teaching in the public schools.

16. Have generations and generations of children spend their entire primary and secondary educations in schools taught by people like these. Have the children hear nothing their entire lives except the superiority of culture A and the absolute worthlessness of culture B.

17. Have those children graduate into a poor economy and find themselves marginalized, frustrated, and resentful.

18. Have those children blame the other group for their misfortunes and vow to take restorative measures to reestablish social decency to the world.

You can see how these steps would lead to enduring ethnic hostility that could last for generations.

Things get more vitriolic if

1B. There are frustrated intellectuals in the other ethnic group who cannot get jobs.

2B. Those intellectuals start schools themselves.

Lange documents this process for many nations. You can read the details yourself in his book *Educations in Ethnic Violence.*

But let me illustrate these arguments with Lange's example of Sri Lanka.

Sri Lanka is an island at the southern tip of India. It is divided between Sinhalese who are Buddhist (76%) and Tamils who are Hindu (17%) (the remaining 7% are other ethnic groups). There were several bouts of ethnic violence between Sinhalese and Tamils after 1956, including a civil war that ran for twenty-six years. Education rates were high in Sri Lanka, with a long tradition of good colonial schools that taught in English, and missionary schools and public schools that taught in Sinhalese or Tamil. Schools segregated Sinhalese and Tamils and taught in only one language. Sinhalese schools taught the wonders of Sinhalese culture and history. Tamil schools taught the wonders of Tamil culture and history. The historical events covered in each school would often be completely different. The social separation of students would continue into university life, where even though universities were mixed, students would split into Sinhalese or Tamil student organizations, each with national political ambitions.

When students graduated, they were often at a tremendous disadvantage compared with uneducated students. The school systems generated huge numbers of graduates, but the economy had mostly working-class and menial offerings. Unemployment was generally three times higher for students who had passed their O-levels (the equivalent of high school juniors) than it was for the uneducated; the gap got increasingly worse over time. Students came to depend on government jobs; they were very vested in having those jobs restricted to members of their own group. The all-Sinhalese or all-Tamil nature of their curricula gave students "excellent" reasons for seeing the other group as unqualified. It motivated all-out social mobilizing to drive the other group out of government work.

However, school is not the only factor that causes conflict. People also respond to the economic realities of how they make a living as adults. Landlessness stimulates all sorts of conflict—ethnic, revolutionary, or warlordist. School may predispose to conflict. Landlessness activates that potential.

Chapter 38

LANDLESSNESS AND POLITICAL VIOLENCE

Not all violent conflict is ethnic.

Nor does all conflict come from hatred, whether socially manufactured or not.

Many violent conflicts are economic. They are fought over issues of money or livelihood. Economic realities also determine whether parties have the strategic capacity to fight.

One of the most important economic circumstances causing conflict is landlessness. The basic idea comes from a classic of 1970's macrosociology, Jeffery Paige's *Agrarian Revolution*. Paige did a statistical analysis of rural insurrections worldwide and found that the areas where small farmers owned their own land were far more stable than areas where farmers were landless.

Technically, small cultivators who own their own land are called *peasants*. Small cultivators who are landless are known as *rural proletariats*. Rural proletariats have no land, so if they want to farm, they have to work for someone else. A migratory harvest worker is a standard example. Why are peasants more conservative than rural proletariats?

1. *Peasants own land and have something to lose. Rural proletariats have nothing so they can take more risks.* If your land means everything to you, why would you want to risk getting in trouble with the authorities and losing the one thing that really matters to you?

2. *Peasants have to take care of their farms. They can't just disappear to go off and fight. Rural proletariats can go anywhere so long as who they are fighting for is keeping them and their families fed.* People who have farms that they don't want to lose have to take care of their crops. For peasants with rice paddies, this can mean nearly constant cultivation, filling and draining the paddies, and weeding the rice. In a temperate climate, farmers need to be around in spring to plow and plant and around in early fall to bring in the harvest.

3. *Peasants live isolated from each other, while rural proletariats have close relationships of friendship and solidarity.* When you own a family farm, this means you live in a farmhouse surrounded by a decent amount of land. The neighbors are far away because both your land and their land are between your houses. You do your work with the members of your family. Your family is who you see.

   When you are a rural proletariat, you typically have a crew of people you work with. Maybe they are the other employees on the farm. Maybe they are the people on your picking crew who ride with you on the truck from place to place.

   When you are isolated from your neighbors, they have no claims on you. If some neighbor asks a peasant to join a political movement, it is like a stranger asking them to join. That stranger would have to be very convincing.

   When you have a team of people you work with, the members of your team *do* have a claim on you. Friends have obligations to each other. Friends help each other out. So when a coworker asks a rural proletariat, very real peer pressure is involved. The rural proletariat will have a harder time saying no.

4. *Peasants compete with each other. Rural proletariats cooperate with each other.* The worst enemies of peasants are often the next-door neighbors. Peasants, if they are going to be rich, need more land. If their farm is going to expand, they will have to take land from the

neighbor on the north, the south, the east, or the west. Your neighbors also have expansion plans. Most of those plans go right through you. Peasants are not naturally "all on the same side." What is hell for the neighbors can be heaven for you. If your neighbor's misfortunes cause them to have to unload land in a distress sale, this can be a once-in-a-lifetime opportunity for you.

It does not help that peasants need to have other farmers fail to get good prices. If you as a farmer have a bumper crop, and all your neighbors and everyone else in the world have bumper crops as well, prices will be rock bottom. Ideally you want a bumper crop for yourself and crop failures for all your neighbors and distant rivals. Then you have a ton of goods to sell, and because the goods are scarce, you can get top dollar for every crateful.

These conflicts of interest make peasant villages notorious for internal disputes and lawsuits. Going to court over inheritances or boundaries is common. Disputes over everything last years and years.

The motivations of rural proletariats are different. When one wins, everybody wins. When one loses, everybody loses. If a grower wants to cut the payments to a harvester, that is a threat that could be used against anyone. Likewise, if one harvester gets aggressive and demands a higher pay rate, that higher rate will apply to all. Rural proletariats are quick to understand the concept of teamwork. If they work together, they all benefit.

What does this imply for social conflict?

If one peasant were to ask another to join a social movement, that other peasant will be reluctant to help out. He may ask, "Why is this guy trying to get me in trouble with the authorities?"

Crews of proletarianized workers in contrast are natural combat squads. They are used to standing up for each other. They will take risks for each other in battle. They will do what it takes to see that the whole group gets taken care of.

If they feel threatened by a predatory landlord, they may join a revolutionary movement.

If they feel threatened by narcotraffickers, they may join a band of vigilantes.

If they are offered inducements to fight guerillas, they may join a death squad.

If they feel threatened by migrants, they may join an ethnic street mob.

Owning land keeps peasants out of violent movements. When they are landless, anything can happen.

Chapter 39

Landlessness and Political Violence

The Evidence

There are a multitude of examples of landlessness leading to political violence. We already saw how the desertification of the Sahel, the Horn of Africa, Yemen, Syria, Iraq, and Afghanistan led to the rise of insurgent movements there.

Statistically, if you compare national rates of civil warfare or violent political uprisings across nations with different levels of land inequality, there is a U-shaped relationship. The most egalitarian nations have very low rates of internal political violence. As land inequality increases, the rate of political insurrections steadily increases. However, at very high levels, the rate goes back down again. The standard interpretation is that at very high levels of land inequality, all of the power is held by a very small elite of super-landlords. They can easily crush any resistance they encounter, so it is no longer viable for poor people to protest.

Superficially, it would seem from this that landlessness wouldn't be a problem. Just let a small set of oligarchs control all the land and they will

be able to keep a lid on everything. The problem is that most of the processes that cause landlessness today destabilize conservatives who would
normally be forces for social control. Land grabs by foreign investors di-
lute the power of national elites. Urban investors or military men buying/
taking land for projects such as mines, plantations, or industrial parks
become political rivals of local established families. Desertification undercuts the economic power of everyone in the ecologically threatened region. This includes the old elites. So, while it may be the case that very
unequal places that have always been unequal are stable. However new
land grabs and increases in land inequality will nearly always promote
greater instability.

Within-nation studies provide further evidence of the destabilizing effects
of landlessness. Landlessness correlates with terrorist attacks among provinces
in Pakistan. This study is particularly interesting because the effect is independent of poverty (which increases terrorism) and the presence of funda-
mentalist Islamic schools. (The schools do not have an effect).

Land inequality is statistically correlated with land invasions in Brazil and
guerilla activity in Colombia.

Sumatra, in Indonesia, has a long history of large foreign-owned plantations granted by the Dutch. During World War II, when the Japanese removed the Dutch, landless workers used the power vacuum to reoccupy many
of the former rubber and tobacco plantations. They did not conveniently leave
when the Dutch returned, nor did they leave when Indonesia became independent. The landless workers had formed a large number of peasant unions,
and these unions fought hard to get land transferred to the local residents.
Those struggles were still occurring in the 2010s. The ownership and legal
structure of the plantation holdings have changed. In the province of Northern Sumatra alone, there are over thirty cases a year of violence or missing
persons related to land disputes.

Note that not all conflict associated with landlessness takes the form of
struggles over land. Rural proletariats are bigger risk takers than are landed
peasants, because they have no land to lose. This means they can fight over
anything that makes them unhappy. A good example of this is how the Arab
Spring played out in Tunisia.

The Arab Spring was a large wave of popular protest that swept through
North Africa and much of the Middle East in 2010. In Tunisia, many groups

rose up, including miners in the south, urban residents in Tunis, and the farmers in the northwest of the country.

Land grabs were occurring as the Tunisian government was reorienting agricultural production away from domestic food production and more toward large export agriculture targeted at European Union markets. However, a larger source of landlessness was the growing demographic unsustainability of the Tunisian farm economy. Population growth, rising costs, and declining prices paid to farmers were making the domestic Tunisian farm economy unsustainable. An increasingly large percentage of the population was being forced to turn to rural nonagricultural wage employment as an expedient in order to survive. The diminished carrying capacity of family farms was making the rural population de facto landless since their sustenance was no longer coming from the land, they were no longer isolated at home away from other rural residents, and they were now wage workers with cooperative rather than competitive incentive structures.

The farmers had complaints about land; state farms were being sold off to large private investors bypassing needy local farmers. However, these were not the primary grievances of the rural protesters in Tunisia's northwest.

They were upset about changes in the state credit system that was depriving them of agricultural loans they needed. They were upset about the privatization of the water system giving them lower supplies of more expensive water. They were upset about the cost of living. As the Tunisian government intentionally increased the percentage of food from imported sources, the cost of purchased food was increasing, materially worsening the farmers' standards of living. Farmers resented the rise of new yuppies in Tunisia who were getting rich while rural people suffered.

They had marches. They had demonstrations. They attacked over one hundred urban-owned or corporate farms. The tactic of choice was to blockade the new owners' barns so that the yuppies would be unable to do spring plowing.

The Arab Spring was successful in Tunisia. The old government fell. A new government emerged that was committed to reform. Like many other governments born of popular dissent, the new regime had a lukewarm commitment to significant change. However, the expansion of corporate farming was significantly slowed with the arrival of democracy. The farmers won a significant partial victory.

The list of examples provided here of landless farmers being involved in protest and agitation is just a sample of what could have been provided. I could have looked at the agrarian histories of any of the nations that appeared as cases in the statistical studies to obtain further anecdotal materials.

Landlessness is destabilizing. The world is becoming more landless.

Chapter 40

The Global Land Grab

Landlessness causes conflict and political instability.

Unfortunately, the amount of landlessness in the world is going up dramatically.

The primary cause for this is a wave of land acquisition in the Global South. China has obtained vast tracts of land in sub-Saharan Africa, Southeast Asia, and Latin America. American, European, and Indian investors are also in the mix. Local elites are in the game as well. They are at least as active as the foreigners in land acquisitions.

Some of the land sales are for bona fide development projects.

Some of the land sales are for investors preparing for the agriculture of tomorrow.

Some of the land sales are completely idle speculation with no plans other than to flip the land to another investor.

Whether for good reasons or bad reasons, lots of land is being sold in the Global South. Cultivators are losing their homes and their livelihoods.

Table 40.1. Known land sales in hectares by nation: Global South, 2000–2019 (nations with at least 200,000 hectares in sales)

Angola	361,730	Malaysia	5,419,744
Argentina	4,146,625	Mali	570,842
Brazil	7,510,701	Mexico	459,342
Burkina Faso	878,459	Mongolia	345,205
Cambodia	1,591,471	Morocco	705,510
Cameroon	770,184	Mozambique	3,027,191
Central African Rep.	1,388,354	Myanmar	1,198,007
Chile	716,693	Nicaragua	519,300
China	1,098,946	Niger	326,100
Colombia	574,031	Nigeria	954,369
Congo, Dem. Rep.	10,588,513	Papua New Guinea	4,112,207
Congo, Rep.	2,242,846	Paraguay	1,084,959
Côte d'Ivoire	260,769	Peru	16,908,241
Ecuador	294,454	Philippines	309,634
Ethiopia	1,447,101	Senegal	371,733
Gabon	2,750,248	Sierra Leone	1,232,911
Ghana	1,129,769	South Africa	438,719
Guatemala	743,654	South Sudan	2,571,982
Guinea	559,049	Sudan	762,208
Guyana	1,376,385	Tanzania	735,859
Indonesia	4,651,746	Uganda	248,033
Kenya	425,070	Uruguay	1,160,470
Lao PDR	930,447	Vietnam	560,107
Liberia	2,559,162	Zambia	1,158,057
Madagascar	1,348,052	Zimbabwe	486,124

Table 40.1 illustrates the sheer magnitude of recent land transfers. There are fifty nations in the table. Nearly twenty of them have sales of over one million hectares. Peru was the leader with nearly seventeen million hectares being transferred. The figures here are probably substantial underestimates. They only include sales for which some official documentation could be found in official government records. Land records in many countries are highly inaccurate with vast omissions. Investors hide land deals to avoid taxation. On the other hand, any plot of land that was sold more than once appears multiple times in these statistics. This could lead to overcounts.

Hectares alone do not always give an accurate impression of the extent of land transfer that is going on. After all, one million hectares means less in Brazil, which is an enormous country, than it does in Lesotho, which is very small. One can also look at land sales as a proportion of the total amount of arable land in a country.

In most countries, the transferred land represents a relatively small percentage of total arable land—often less than 5 percent. However, this is not always the case.

Table 40.2 lists the countries where the land sales from 2000 to 2019 represented at least a third of the total arable land area in a country. One-third of the total arable land area in a country is a huge amount. Ten countries experienced such massive land transfers. Some were in Africa: the Democratic Republic of the Congo, Gabon, Liberia, and Sierra Leone. Some were in South America, such as Peru and Uruguay. Some were in Southeast Asia or Oceania, such as Malaysia and Papua New Guinea.

Note that the table is not showing that one-third of the arable land was actually sold. It says that a quantity of land *equal to* one-third of the arable land was sold. Many land sales involve nonagricultural land. This would certainly be the case in Malaysia or Papua New Guinea, where many of the land sales involve forest or mountain land for mining, lumbering, or energy projects. Farmland might be completely left alone while all the dispossession occurs out on the frontier.

Table 40.2. Countries where land sales represented at least a third of the area of total arable land, 2000–2019

Democratic Republic of the Congo
Republic of the Congo
Gabon
Guyana
People's Democratic Republic of Laos
Liberia
Malaysia
Papua New Guinea
Peru
Sierra Leone
South Sudan
Uruguay

The fact that land transfers do not involve what is officially designated as "arable" land does not mean that dispossession is not occurring. Frontier areas are populated by indigenous people. Their informal methods of gathering or slash-and-burn horticulture are often not treated as agriculture by official economic censuses. Don't think for a minute that dispossessing indigenous peoples is a completely peaceful process that leads to neither war nor violence. When the United States occupied Native American lands, none of that territory officially counted in the census as "arable" land, since the frontier was not cultivated by white people. Those land seizures led to three hundred years of Indian wars.

Is land acquisition always violent? Jasmin Hristov's work on paramilitaries suggests a widespread pattern of forcible eviction. However, a large proportion of land transfers are amicable. One party wants to buy land and offers a good price. The other party happily takes the deal. Plenty of economic transactions are win-win. Michael Levien documents completely voluntaristic high-price land sales in his book on land dispossession in India. Voluntaristic deals may produce good outcomes, but this is not always the case. Levien's ex-farmers, who got the good deals, still ended up being economically wiped out. His farmers, like many others, lacked the skills to get any kind of lucrative job in an urban economy. The farmers found themselves unemployed, or working as sweepers or cleaners. They went from being somewhat poor to deeply impoverished.

Note that we should be careful about assigning 100 percent of the blame for landlessness to "evil capitalists." Many rural individuals would be driven into landlessness and poverty even if transfers of land were occurring. Let's now consider the causes of landlessness that are based on simple normal routine considerations.

Chapter 41

POPULATION GROWTH AND LANDLESSNESS

Not all landlessness comes from land grabs.

If the population grows rapidly, a lot of landlessness will occur naturally.

Imagine a small plot of land that will support a farmer and his wife. What happens if they have four children? Not all of them can live on the land. Either the land becomes divided among all the children, giving them plots that are too small to be viable, or the land goes to one of the children and his or her spouse. The other three children will have to find some other way to survive. When birthrates are high, there is an enormous number of children to take care of. Many will become landless, even if official land policies are as beneficent as can be humanly imagined.

Ecologically oriented readers likely have already noticed that population growth produces a lot more problems than mere landlessness. The more people that exist, the more the earth's resources get consumed by human beings. We use more water, fish more fish, burn more energy, and consume more nonrenewable minerals and hydrocarbons. We cut down more forests and pollute more air. The more people there are on the planet, the more damage we do to the environment. This is a very serious threat in and of itself.

Ecological destruction creates more landlessness. As we destroy the various ecological niches of the planet, we make it difficult for people to subsist on them. Recall the early chapter on desertification and terrorism. The Sahara desert continues to creep southward. Population growth puts too many people and herds on fragile semiarid land. The herds eat the ground cover, the land can no longer retain water, and a previously viable farming and herding region becomes a desert. The residents become landless and turn to crime and warlordism.

So what are the prospects for controlling the size of the world population? Sadly, the projections are not good. Consider the following table.

As of 2019, the world has a population of 7,713 million people. There has been dramatic growth in the past seventy years. In 1950, there were only 2,536 million people. The size of the world population has tripled since then. The world population is expected to stabilize by 2100, at a size of 10,875 million. That means we will be adding roughly 50 percent to the world population, all of whom will need to be fed and provided for.

The drain this will represent on world food and energy supplies is obvious. Less obvious but just as important is what this will do to landlessness. The world land supply is not going to go up by 50 percent. It could expand somewhat with deforestation. We know the general ecological effects of deforestation.

So the future prospects for the percentage of the population in the Global South will be landless are pretty grim.

Table 41.1. World population estimates by year

Year	Population size (in millions)
1950	2,536
1975	4,079
2000	6,143
2025 (est.)	8,184
2050 (est.)	9,735
2075 (est.)	10,577
2100 (est.)	10,875

"Wait a minute!" some readers will say. "Hasn't fertility gone down? Don't we now have access to modern contraception? Aren't women becoming increasingly liberated? Aren't women becoming more educated and participating more extensively in the labor force? Won't this lead to women having fewer children, providing a basic solution to the population growth problem?"

Well, yes and no.

Individual women are having fewer children. Professional demographers use sophisticated mathematical techniques to measure this process. But simple crude birthrates tell the story perfectly well. Crude birthrates measure the number of births per thousand population. Those rates have been declining dramatically, for all the reasons given previously: contraception, feminism, greater female education, and greater female labor force participation.

Table 41.2 shows the crude birthrates for five-year periods (those are five-year periods and not six-year periods because they count only the last half of the first year and the first half of the last year). You can see that the birthrates are falling, falling, falling. Individual women are having fewer children than they have ever had in history.

So what's the problem? The number of women having births keeps going up, even if each individual woman is having fewer children. If a mother and a father (two people) have three surviving children (three people), then each successive generation is 50 percent larger than the one that went before it. This produces larger and larger numbers of girls, most of whom will have children when they become adults.

Table 41.3 shows how this has operated between 1950 and the present day. Even though birthrates have been steadily declining between 1950 and 2020, the number of births each year continues to increase. The most recent five-year period had 43 percent more births than the world had in 1950–1955, before the onset of fertility reduction in the Global South. That continued high

Table 41.2. World crude birthrates by year

Years	Births per 1,000 population
1950–1955	36.9
1975–1980	28.5
2000–2005	21.0
2015–2020	18.0

Table 41.3. World number of births by year

Years	Births (in millions)
1950 1955	490
1975–1980	608
2000–2005	667
2015–2020	701

number of births is what ensures that the world population will continue to increase all the way through 2100.

This means the prospects for landlessness are grim.

It also means the prospects for resource depletion and ecological destruction are also grim.

Controlling the size of the world population is extremely important. Using contraception and delayed marriage to reduce the number of births is a much more appealing solution than having the population reduced by war, famine, or catastrophic plague.

Chapter 42

Triggers of Destruction

We have discussed a wide variety of factors that lead to societal dysfunction: crime, corruption, weakening of state capacity to support the economy. These are all serious problems. When our society starts declining, these will all be symptoms of our larger decay—and aggravating considerations that accelerate the rate of overall decline.

But frankly, right now, the world is doing fairly well. GDP capita has been steadily increasing. These increases have occurred in both the Global North and the Global South. Mortality rates continue to fall. Science continues to advance.

Steven Pinker writes relentlessly optimistic books about the positive trajectory of the modern world. If you look at most indicators of social progress, his optimism is fully justified.

Yet societies do die. At some point, something triggers a negative force that reverses the direction of evolution. What went up starts going down.

What are the plausible triggers that could start a process of societal devolution? No one knows exactly what will take down the current Euro-

American world system. But I list some plausible candidates for triggers here. The top items strike me as the most probable and alarming. The other items could be problematic as well. However, they are less likely to produce catastrophic consequences. The dynamics of each trigger are explained in the subsequent chapters. But here are some of the danger areas to worry about:

1. *Downturns in the Mensch cycle.* The global economy has long-term cycles that alternate between booms that last for decades and busts that last for decades. Enduring recessions and depressions are a regular feature of capitalism. They are based on cycles of technological innovation and stagnation. The busts generally resolve themselves naturally. However, these economic downturns trigger all sorts of negative social forces.

2. *Ecological disasters.* The steady advance of the modern industrial world system has been based on an environment that has posed no significant limits to expansion. When we ran out of resources, we just went to new places and got more resources. What happens if we actually run out of something for good, or create an adverse natural obstacle that becomes impossible to control?

3. *Landlessness-based violence.* Social conflict is the result of perceived threat. That perception can be based on reality. Violence decreases people's willingness to cooperate at a global level. It also increases people's willingness to use violence themselves. There may be slow, subtle reductions in global capacity based on nations' refusals to cooperate with each other. Military action can also lead to its own catastrophic consequences.

4. *Increase in patriarchy.* The world has lived and grown while tolerating enormous levels of patriarchy. Furthermore, gender equality has been advancing globally, despite setbacks in particular places on issues such as abortion rights. The increase in women's education, women's economic activity, and women's power within the family has led to a wide variety of social benefits including increased economic growth, lower population growth, and reduced participation in civil war. As long as the trend toward gender equality continues, the world will continue to receive the benefits of greater prosperity, fewer population pressures on the environment, and relative peace.

But what would happen if patriarchy were to regain the upper hand and the trend in gender equality were to stall or reverse?

Downturns in Mensch cycles are inevitable. Ecological hazards are harder to predict, but it is unlikely that the world faces absolutely no environmental threats whatsoever. The world is already experiencing more frequent and intense low-level wars from increased landlessness. Will that lead to something more serious? Who can say? A global snapback to traditional patriarchy seems unlikely. But this process is occurring in more localized areas. In those settings, the effects of the limitation of women's activity have already led to significant damage.

Let's consider the trigger dynamics in greater detail.

Chapter 43

Long-Term Booms and Busts in Capitalism

Economic growth is not a guaranteed thing. While there has been a general upward trend in GDP and standards of living, there have been constant recessions and depressions along the way. Some of the recessions are passing; others are more severe and tend to go on forever.

When the economy is bad, nothing else seems to work. Governments become ineffective, because (1) they have no money and (2) there are usually other causes of the depression, which the government can't do much about. People become cynical. People become distrustful. Ethnic hostility goes up. Government leaders start looking for military adventures to cover for their lack of success in the economic sphere. All in all, long depressions make everything else bad.

Recessions and depressions are frequent phenomena because economic growth at the global level is loosely cyclical. Periods of prosperity alternate with periods of major downturns. The most famous theory of cycles comes from the Soviet economist Nikolai Kondratieff, who posited fifty-year cycles of twenty-five years of boom and twenty-five years of bust. There are lots of reasons to be skeptical of a tight 25/25 characterization. Some nations are not on the same rhythm as the rest of the world. Some booms and busts don't start exactly when a twenty-five-year prediction says they should. But the basic long-cycle phenomenon of Kondratieff waves is real and has a lot to do with when depressions occur.

My own personal favorite of long cycles is technological and comes from the work of Gerhard Mensch. In fact, I prefer to talk about Mensch waves rather than Kondratieff waves (although I use both terms).

But as good as Mensch is, Mensch is not the entire story. There are global factors that matter as well. Let's look at the five big Kondratieff waves and then deal with the factors that caused them (see table 43.1).

The Industrial Revolution—which was the origin of the prosperity we now enjoy in the modern world—was really a case of new product development. Previously, clothing had been handmade, making it very expensive. Machine spinning and weaving dropped the price of clothing dramatically; now even poor people could afford whole wardrobes. The world went on a clothes-buying binge, leading to one of the greatest economic expansions in history. The clothes-buying binge began to fade in the 1820s. The British and world economy, however, were rescued by railways.

The building of the railways was a tremendous source of world growth in the 1840s and 1850s (although some important lines had been built before then). Nearly every major city was connected with everywhere else in the world. The railway boom required not only the buying of a lot of land and the laying of a lot of rails. It required constructing vast numbers of railway engines and passenger cars, building railway stations in every city, and

Table 43.1. The five great Kondratieff waves

Cycle number	Boom	Bust	Product base
I	1790–1820	1820–1840	Machine textiles
II	1840–1870	1870–1890	Railroads
III	1890–1920	1920–1940	Structural steel
IV	1940–1970	1970–1990	Automobiles
V	1990–?	?	Computer/internet

digging enough coal mines to keep all those steam engines running. Ultimately, this boom too ran its course. All the lines that made sense had been built, and subsequent lines were money losers. Then the world economy was rescued again—by structural steel.

The invention of modern steel led to a reconstruction of every large structure in the developed world. Wood buildings became steel-framed buildings. Wood boats and bridges became iron boats and bridges. Cheap, high-quality steel facilitated the use of heavy machinery and large amounts of wire, paving the way for the electrical revolution. Unfortunately, much of the transformation of world structures from wood to steel had been accomplished by 1920. The 1920s saw depression throughout Europe, followed by the Great Depression of the 1930s. Then the world economy was rescued again—by the automobile.

Every family came to own a car, and later on, two cars. The automobiles were rapidly replaced as technology improved. Cars with hand cranks became cars with keyed ignitions. Cars with manual brakes became cars with power brakes.

Furthermore, the automobile generated a huge number of by-product industries. Highways had to be built to accommodate the new vehicles. The cars needed gasoline—dramatically expanding the petroleum industry. Cars made commuting to work feasible, making it possible for people to live in suburbs and drive to the city. This led to a complete restructuring of world cities with the creation of vast new suburbs and the shopping facilities to go with them. Restaurants became economically viable as an industry; people might not walk fifteen miles to have a fried clam dinner, but they would drive fifteen miles to have a fried clam dinner. The insurance industry thrived since all of the vehicles needed to be insured.

Ultimately, however, shoppers in the developed world had all the cars they needed. Worse, the great new innovations stopped coming, so there was no need for people to jettison older-generation cars for better models. The saturated market made the 1970s and 1980s years of economic stagnation and slow global growth. The world economy was saved again—this time by the personal computer and the internet.

You probably know the history of the computer/internet era. There is no need to review it here. Every time Google or Apple or Microsoft or upstart unicorns come up with a new product that is a big hit, that is a sign that the fifth Kondratieff wave is alive and well. If you see long strings of new product rollouts that do nothing, represent trivial improvements over what is already out there, and generate little public interest or sales, start worrying. A long run of product busts with no countervailing big hits is a mark that the era of technological stagnation may have arrived.

Chapter 44

Technological and International Causes of Stagnation

The long-term booms and busts of capitalism are driven by two dynamics: those of technology and those of international competition.

Technological Cycles

Mensch argued that Kondratieff waves are driven by natural cycles in the advance and stagnation of science. Economic development is dependent on having new products to sell. Mensch argued that the great expansionary cycles of the world were linked to fundamental technological innovations that generated a broad range of related products. Busts occur when the engineering of a given product becomes so well understood that no new improvements can be made.

Cycles start with a breakthrough innovation such as factories that can make cheap clothes or assembly lines that can make cheap cars. The new breakthrough creates a product that everyone wants. A huge number of sales are linked to people acquiring the product for the first time.

The new product produces collateral growth through multipliers. The textile factories and the auto factories need supplies. Cotton growers in the Industrial Revolution and steel makers in the auto age got rich supplying the new factories. The workers in the factories also stimulated the economy with the consumer purchases they were making with their wages. The breakthrough product thus provides a triple boom: a boom in the core product itself, a boom for the industrial suppliers, and a boom for the people who make consumption goods for workers.

The excitement over the new product attracts new engineers into the relevant industry. This new talent looks for ways to improve the product. The automobiles of Henry Ford's day were not very good. They could not go very fast and were hard to drive. They had to be started with a hand crank. Engineers found lots of ways to make the new product even better. They invented keyed ignitions, bigger engines, automatic transmissions, power steering, and power brakes.

Everyone replaced their old vehicles with new vehicles. This meant new sales from all the people who had bought cars originally. These new sales had multipliers too. So, there were booms for all the industrial suppliers as well as the makers of consumer goods.

The party ends when the engineers run out of ideas. In the 1970s, the automobile industry went stale. The 1950s and 1960s saw the invention of power steering, power brakes, and convertibles. These were big sellers. After that, Detroit would come up with no more blockbuster ideas until the SUV boom of the 1990s.

Technological stagnation does not kill industries, but it does cripple them. Industries can survive replacing worn-out goods with new goods. But this does not create nearly the volume of sales that comes from hot new products. An economy without major innovation will have mediocre growth rates.

Growth will stay mediocre until some new breakthrough innovation comes. If the breakthrough innovation doesn't happen, then capitalism can go into long-term stagnation. There is no cosmic law guaranteeing breakthrough innovations occur.

The Global Dynamics of Cycles

In Mensch's world, the entire world gained equally or lost equally from the dynamics of technological cycles. In the real world, technology is a tool of domination where scientifically strong nations drain the scientifically weak. During periods of technological innovation, the rich world gains at the expense of the poorer nations. When technological innovation is stagnant, the poor nations get their revenge. Wealth accrues to the Global South at the expense of the Global North.

During the period of technological advance, the country creating new and desirable products obtains a strategic monopoly. This sets up conditions of *unequal terms of trade*. The innovating nation can charge top dollar for its new goods. The rest of the world does not have this advantage. The result is that money flows from the rest of the world to the innovating nation.

Second- and third-wave innovations are more evenly dispersed. Any nation that can generate a reasonably sized population of engineers can find small improvements to make to a preexisting product. This means the nation that once had a monopoly will now live in a world where these profits have to be shared. Money will continue to accrue to the original breakthrough nation, but other nations will receive income flows as well.

Generally, only developed nations will have the engineering capacity to make these second- and third-generation innovations. The underdeveloped world will still be out of the game. The rich nations as a whole will experience unequal terms of exchange in comparison with the poor nations; money will flow from the Global South to the Global North, with the advantage of the original innovator being less apparent.

Unfortunately for the rich nations, no scientific monopoly remains a monopoly forever. There are lots of ways for poor nations to learn rare skills. They can hire engineers from the wealthy nation to work in their own country. They can send their own students to learn engineering in rich nations and then come home. They can buy the monopoly product and reverse engineer it. If need be, they can just start a company to build the scarce product and try and try again until they finally figure out how to make it. Nothing stays a secret forever.

Once technology is stagnant and the skills to produce products have become widely dispersed, then competition is based on price rather than quality. If everyone can make a standard good, the only question is, Who can make it cheaper? Now all the advantages accrue to the poor nations:

1. Wages are lower in the poor nations. Low labor costs guarantee that the underdeveloped nations will win the price war.
2. The nations that enter an industry last will have the newest, best equipment. The last player in the game is frequently the most productive.
3. Manufacturers in the rich nations will find it makes sense to move production from their own countries to the underdeveloped nations because nearly every factor of production will be cheaper in the poorer economy.

The Mensch dynamics and the global dynamics hit at exactly the same time. So just as the rich nations are running out of sales due to technological stagnation, lots of low-cost competitors appear to fight for whatever sales are left. The rich nations are hit with a double whammy; the recessions that come out of this double threat can be massive.

Chapter 45

Will There Be a Sixth Mensch Cycle?

There have been five Mensch cycles (or if you prefer the more traditional term, Kondratieff cycles). There have been cycles for textiles, railroads, steel, automobiles, and computers, respectively. When the first four major products died, after long periods of stagnation, a new product emerged to revitalize the world economy.

After the fifth Mensch cycle—personal computers and the internet—finally dies, will there be a sixth Mensch cycle to reestablish the global economy?

Nobody knows.

It is difficult to know what the next big product will be. In the textile factory era, railways only existed in mines to help bring heavy ore from the mine face to the outside. No one imagined it would become the dominant form of transportation for the century. In the steel era, no one imagined that horseless carriages would be a serious product. No one could see that the automobile would be the great creation of the twentieth century.

It is also difficult to know what country will invent the next great innovation. England invented the key products of the first two Mensch cycles: textile factories and railways. The great innovation of the third cycle, steel, was jointly developed by the United States and Germany, leaving England out in the cold. The United States developed the innovations for the fourth and fifth Mensch cycles, automobiles and computers. The fact that the United States was the developer of the key product in three out of the last three Mensch cycles explains why America is the dominant economic and political force in the world today.

But will the next great innovation come from the United States? Or will it come from China? Or will it come from the excellent scientists that work in Russia? Or will it come from the European Union? No one knows what that product will be, and no one knows where that product will be developed.

No one knows if a product worthy of a sixth Mensch cycle will even exist. Most of history has not seen breakthrough inventions every fifty years. The period from 1790 to 2020 was an exception. Who is to say that the historical forces of 1500 BC–AD 1789 will not reestablish themselves?

If the United States wants there to be a sixth Mensch cycle, and if it wants the key invention to be developed in the United States, then protecting and maintaining America's scientific capacity is essential. The United States became technologically superior because it had the best research universities in the world. The world is now heavily invested in catching up to the United States. Will a future America be forced into economic and technological submission by a country that can make strategic goods that we simply can't replicate?

The ownership of science means the ownership of the Mensch cycle. Right now, our technological advantage is quite substantial. Whether we will keep that advantage in the future is very much an open question.

Chapter 46

EVER-EXPANDING FRONTIERS
OF ECOLOGICAL DESTRUCTION

So far, we have talked little about ecological destruction. In chapter 10, there were illustrations of civilizations that died from destroying their environments. The counterresponse was to invoke ecological modernization, the process by which societies find technical solutions to ecological issues. There are cases, like the cleanup of the Great Lakes, where societies really do confront their environmental issues head-on and find solutions. There are also cases where ecological problems kill. Betting on ecological modernization is like betting on the New York Yankees to win on a given Thursday. The Yankees win often. Often is not always.

There are multiple forces that predispose capitalism to ever-increasing amounts of environmental damage. Sociologists discuss the *treadmill of production*, the degradation of the biosphere coming from increasing population growth and GDP requiring consuming ever-greater amounts of natural resources.

A more refined argument is *expanding frontiers of production*. Modern economies require the incorporation of ever-greater amounts of physical space into capitalist production. Whenever an area is converted to commercial use, its natural function gets destroyed. Consider real estate development. As cities expand, fields and natural habitats are destroyed to create buildings that can be sold.

Expanding frontiers of production occur on a grander scale internationally. Consider natural resource extraction. Early resource extraction takes place in convenient locations near preexisting centers of population. As the early, easy deposits get exhausted, extraction has to move to more remote and more distant locations. In the United States, the earliest petroleum development was in Pennsylvania—near America's largest cities. As Pennsylvania ran dry, the oil companies had to move their operations to Texas. After Texas came the Middle East. After the Middle East came the North Sea and northern Alaska. Now, there is exploration in the middle of the South Atlantic. Each location is more inconvenient, is more expensive, and fouls a new part of the environment.

Jason Moore has the grimmest view of economic growth and ecological degradation. He argues that capitalism is dependent on the *four cheaps*:

1. Cheap food
2. Cheap energy
3. Cheap natural resources
4. Cheap labor

All four are subject to expanding frontiers of production. The need to feed Europe's labor force led to the expansion of agriculture in North and South America. The need for cheap labor led to the creation of the transatlantic slave trade. The world keeps expanding and expanding to meet the global economy's endless hunger for the four cheaps. The physical planet gets destroyed in the process.

However, the physical destruction of environments is not the only problem with expanding frontiers of production. The incorporation of new space into capitalist production means the dislocation of the population originally living in that space. The creation of farms in the American West meant removal of the indigenous populations that were living there. This is a violent process. The indigenous population starts out being landed. It ends up being landless. Not only are the newly landless victimized; they are prone to fight back and become violent themselves.

The American Indians fought wars against the Europeans and Americans who wanted to take their lands. These battles were one-sided. The American Indians were crushed.

However, modern military technology has shifted the balance in favor of insurgents. Wilderness rebels now have mortars, antiaircraft missiles, and fully automatic weapons. Wars over land are now more protracted. They are bloodier and offer better prospects for the rebels.

The tactics of guerilla warfare have also been refined. Guerilla warfare existed in earlier periods; Spanish irregulars made life miserable for Napoleon. However, pitched battles on open fields are a thing of the past. Local rebels use mountainous terrain and forest cover to give substantial defensive advantages. (Urban buildings provide equally fine defensive positions.) The Viet Cong and the FARC were impossible to eradicate. It took fifty years for the Philippine government to defeat the Moros in Mindanao.

The rebels may be able to defend themselves. Unarmed residents, not so much. Regardless of their personal positions concerning the rebellion, they are at the mercy of security forces out to kill anyone who "might just be" a rebel. In a war against highland rebels in Guatemala in the 1980s, General Rios Montt took the position that Indians were by definition rebels. His army was instructed to systematically exterminate the Ixil Mayans. They slaughtered over three thousand indigenous people a month, including the complete eradication of over four hundred communities.

Expanding frontiers of production not only means increased destruction of our ecosystem. It also means increased war. The widening scope of production incorporates ever more space into territory allocated for commercial purposes. As land gets "put to good use," the old residents who are not part of those plans become displaced. Landlessness leads to political volatility and warfare.

As Gregory Hooks once said, "War is development in reverse." Military violence wrecks everything. Farms, buildings, and human lives are destroyed. Education is put on hold, as young people have to spend their time fighting. Normal government activity grinds to a halt. Hospitals become hard to maintain. Infrastructure construction is a lost cause when everything is about to be blown up.

The first prerequisite of ecological modernization is peace. If the world is torn up by violence, ecological modernization is torn up as well.

The first prerequisite of having a large web of cooperation is peace. When the bullets start flying, trust turns to fear. Fear leads to hatred. Hatred leads to more conflict.

Chapter 47

Why Women's Power Matters

Our discussion thus far has been completely ungendered. We have been talking about global well-being as if gender differences had nothing to do with this. In fact, women's power is one of the fundamental determinants of not only economic growth but also education levels, ecological sustainability, and social peace. Rae Blumberg, one of the leading writers in gender and development, calls female empowerment a "magic potion" for development.

Women's power does not produce good outcomes because women are the source of all virtue while men are the source of all evil. Nor is it the case that violent, corrupt, predatory women don't exist. There are plenty of female politicians in the Global South who, just like the men, are adept at the arts of realpolitik, calculated brutality, and self-enrichment.

However, statistics show that nations where women are powerful have very substantial advantages:

1. Countries with high levels of female labor force participation or female education are statistically likely to have higher rates of economic growth.
2. Countries where women are relatively empowered have higher rates of education for both genders.
3. Countries with high levels of female labor force participation have more sustainable agriculture and lower levels of pollution.
4. Countries with high levels of female labor force participation are less likely to participate in international wars.

Why does women's power produce social and economic benefit?

A key consideration is that women who are highly educated or have access to their own sources of income have lower fertility. Women with money and career opportunities are less dependent on their husbands for economic survival and can afford to stand up to argue for their own interests. They do not have to provide sexual access on demand; if they do not want to have babies, they don't have them.

What are the benefits of low fertility?

1. Low fertility promotes economic development. In high-fertility nations, between 1961 and 2006, 91 percent of all economic growth went toward feeding an ever-larger population. In countries with lower rates of population growth, growth turns into surplus, which can be invested in further growth.
2. Low fertility increases education levels. In poor nations, schooling is not necessarily free. There can be mandatory fees, transportation costs, and, for secondary students, tutoring for entrance exams. Small families with few children have more money to spend on each child, allowing for more education.
3. Low fertility does not produce more sustainable ecological practices per se. But low population growth does reduce ecological pressures on scarce natural resources.
4. Low fertility reduces crime and internal warfare. When a population grows faster than the economy, the surplus population will be unemployed. Unemployment will be most severe for youth. Teenagers who are poor, don't have jobs, and don't see a future

for themselves are perfect recruiting material for gangs and warlords.

～

Fertility reduction tells part of the story about why empowering women produces social development. However, there are other considerations at work as well.

1. Women's empowerment contributes to economic development in many ways. If women are educated, they become more productive, and the labor force becomes more productive.

    Women's labor force participation is linked to the presence of industries that employ a lot of women. This includes labor-intense export-oriented manufacture. Women are an essential component in the global commodity chains that produce the world's clothing and electronics. This is generally sweatshop labor. However, sweatshops are often a better deal than what existed before. When workers in the rural west of China migrate to the cities to work in sweatshops, it is because the sweatshops pay more than what they could have earned at home. China's industrialization is inconceivable without female labor.

    Women's entrepreneurship also matters. In preindustrial economies, women do trading or grow extra crops or make goods to sell. Blumberg has found that a key determinant of women's economic activity is whether women are allowed to keep the money from their enterprises. When husbands expropriate these profits, this undercuts the financial incentives of the women and causes them to withdraw into passivity.

2. Women's power increases the human capital of future generations. In multiple studies of household consumption in the Global South, women have been shown to be more likely to spend household income on children's education. Men spend more on status goods and immediate consumption.

3. To some extent the relationship between gender equality and a clean environment is a cheat. Women work in industries that are by nature cleaner. Men are more likely to work in heavy industrial sec-

tor settings such as chemical plants, paper plants, petroleum refining, or steel mills. All of these are heavy polluters.

However, there is some evidence that women maintain more ecological practices in agriculture. In farming, women use more traditional methods. These are intrinsically more ecofriendly.

4. The statistical correlation between female social power and reduced warfare is explained in part by the historical record of women participating in peacekeeping activities. Women have been involved in organized peacemaking in Northern Ireland, Bosnia, Nepal, Somalia, South Africa, and Northern Uganda. In Somalia and Mindanao, women have traditionally had peacekeeping roles because they are noncombatants. In Liberia, Leymah Gbowee led a team of women who ended a 2002 civil war, earning Gbowee a Nobel Peace Prize. A study of international peace interventions found that no organized women's groups ever opposed such a peace initiative; if any single-gender groups opposed peace talks, they were generally all-male.

Peacekeeping is probably only a part of the story. Women are mothers who try to protect their children from harm. Women are less likely to resolve interpersonal conflicts with violence. Not every woman is a pacifist, but there may be more nonviolent women than men.

Thus overall, it seems that women's power has a positive effect on human well-being. Over time, women's status has been improving. But is it absolutely guaranteed that the world always progresses in a feminist fashion, and women will be achieving greater and greater equality and autonomy?

Chapter 48

Patriarchy Redux?

Some readers may be somewhat skeptical of the preceding chapter. Historically, the world has become increasingly gender egalitarian. Culture is changing. It seems that the gains made by women in the past two hundred years may be permanent.

Don't get overconfident about women's prospects. A patriarchal backlash is in progress in much of the world. The causes of such a backlash are present now and will reappear in the future. The gains made by women will probably be maintained. But this will not be the case for every nation on the planet. There will be settings where women's power and the beneficent effects associated with such power will get rolled back.

There are two primary mechanisms that could lead to antifeminist backlash. The first is declining male economic status. Leicht and Baker have argued that, globally, men are losing earning power due to deindustrialization in the Global North and rising unemployment in the Global South. Unemployed and underemployed men lose power within their families, particularly if the wife becomes the primary breadwinner. Men react to this loss of status by turning conservative and striving to reconstruct traditional gender roles. This leads to fights against reproductive rights and in favor of traditional religion. Anger and frustration also lead to increased use of violence, which is targeted against both minorities and women.

Blumberg and I have argued that war and crime have similar effects. Warfare and crime prioritize male combativeness and machismo. They put women in danger and make them dependent on the physical protection of men. They limit the ability of women to move freely owing to security concerns. Unfortunately, the deterioration of economies in the Global South pushes men into warlordism and gang life. Male resentment from lost earning power leads to domestic abuse and sexism on its own. It also increases societal violence, which leads to sexual violence and male control of women.

For whatever reason, antifeminism is on the march in much of the world.

In Poland, there is an explicit movement against feminism jointly sponsored by the governing Law and Justice Party and the Catholic Church. The church itself is sponsoring a "STOP GENDER" campaign, with the word "gender" being in English. The implication is that gender is a foreign construct that no nationalist Pole should accept. The government has implemented a policy designed to increase the birthrate by providing cash to women who have babies. The explicit goal is to have more women staying home taking care of children.

Yemen saw a significant rollback of women's rights in the 1990s. South Yemen was a relatively progressive government with a secularized Marxist government. In 1970, gender equality was written into the constitution. In 1974, a law was passed giving women and men equal power within the family. In 1990, South Yemen fell and was reunited with North Yemen. All of the old patriarchal policies were reestablished. Among the most adverse changes: honor killings of women by men were explicitly legalized; women were formally required by law to provide sexual access to their husbands.

In Kenya, a new constitution in 2010 that guaranteed a fixed quota of parliamentary seats for women led to a gigantic backlash of antifeminism. Within the political sphere, the new women candidates were generally marginalized. More disturbingly, there was a substantial increase in political violence channeled against women candidates and their supporters. Crowds and thugs were egged on not only by male political opponents but also by the mass media, which unabashedly refer to female politicians as prostitutes. Women candidates are stripped naked by crowds, slammed into walls while trying to speak, or simply knifed by gangs.

Walsh and Menjivar, two specialists on gendered violence in Central America, report that domestic violence is increasing in that part of the world. Killings of women have increased 400 percent in Honduras between 2002 and 2013. Some of this is due to the increased presence of criminal gangs, which raised both crime rates and homicide rates overall. However, some of this is due to antifeminist backlash. Most of the killings of women in Honduras and El Salvador involve domestic violence rather than gang or criminal activity. The women who Walsh and Menjivar interview report that the police do little to nothing to protect women in danger. In El Salvador, where domestic abuse laws actually exist on the books, only 1.5 percent of the domestic violence cases that are tried in court produce convictions. Keep in mind that the overwhelming majority of cases never come to court in the first place.

In Argentina, violence against women is increasing. The number of homicides with female victims rose over 40 percent between 2008 and 2017. In the 1980s and 1990s women were making significant progress. Divorce was legalized, the use of violence by husbands and fathers was restricted, and quotas were put in for women's parliamentary representation. There has been little significant progress since then. Limits on abortion were made much stricter in 2008. In 2018, the Argentine legislature rejected a bill to decriminalize abortion. There is a significant online presence in Argentina of antifeminist trolls.

Fortunately, while individual countries have seen increases in violence against women, the increase in risk is not worldwide. Global rates of intimate partner female homicide have been stable. Sadly, stable also means not declining. In some countries, base rates of violence against women are very high. Every year in Tanzania, fully one-third of women report being a victim of violence. Ironically, if you ask about wife beating specifically, the figure rises to 70 percent—70 percent every year.

～

Will antifeminism be the number-one factor that causes the end of the world? Probably not. But it can affect the extent to which the world can heal from whatever other shocks it receives.

So now let us consider the larger question.

What causes societies to die?

Chapter 49

The Circle of Societal Death

We have now laid the groundwork for constructing a general model of societal death.

What makes societies die?

It is a twelve-step process, known as the Circle of Societal Death.

Let's consider each step one at a time.

Assume some externally caused source of economic decline. This will lower governmental functioning by lowering tax revenues.

Low Tax
Revenue

↑

Economic
Decline

Low tax revenue reduces the ability of the government to function because it lacks the money to do its job. Government performance drops markedly.

**Poor Government
Performance**
↗
**Low Tax
Revenue**
↑
Economic
Decline

Low government revenues and performance demoralize government functionaries. No budget and no power means government officials can no longer realistically do their jobs.

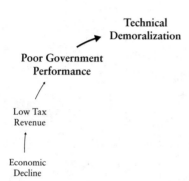

Technical
Demoralization

Poor Government
Performance

Low Tax
Revenue

Economic
Decline

When government officials are powerless and irrelevant, there is no reason for them not to become corrupt. People hold themselves to the highest standards when sticking to the straight and narrow will accomplish something meaningful or valuable. When showing up to the office is a joke, there is no reason not to take bribes. When you can't do anything useful, you may as well protect yourself economically.

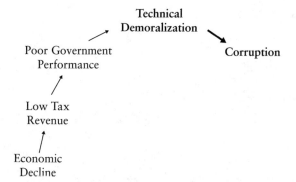

Corruption in the police and the judiciary leads to crime. The crooks pay off the cops. Judges, for a price, will let perpetrators walk.

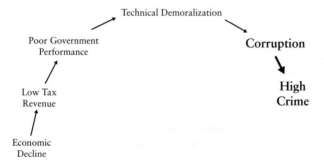

Once people become genuinely worried about personal security, everything else starts falling apart. Societal functioning is dependent on the ability to trust other people. It is particularly dependent on the ability to trust strangers. Once the world becomes a dangerous place, people can count on only a limited number of people. You can only trust people within your small social circle whom you already know. Networks of social cooperation contract.

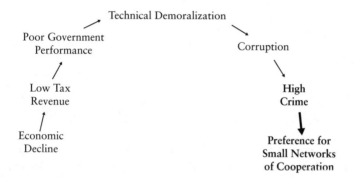

When people only trust people within their own small circle of cooperation, they distrust everyone else. This means they delegitimate everything outside the group, especially the state.

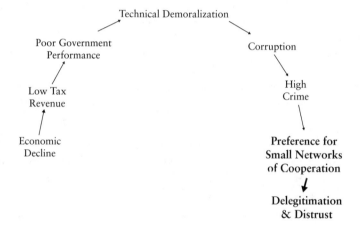

Once people prefer small social networks, everything becomes defined in ethnic terms. Racial and ethnic boundaries are shorthand for defining "us" versus "them." Ethnic discrimination becomes far more prevalent. Ethnic conflict becomes widespread.

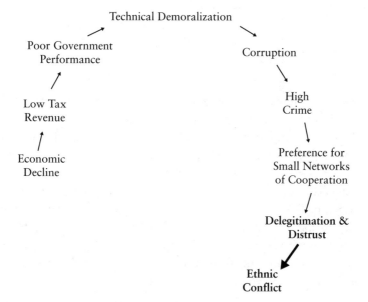

As both crime and ethnic conflict escalate, young people are drawn into self-defense activity. Kids join gangs. They are recruited for armies. Neighborhood youth protect their neighborhoods by forming defense forces and militia. Participation in organized coercion takes them out of more productive activities. They stop their education and drop out of school. They drop out of the labor market and leave their jobs. The more entrepreneurial ones are kept from starting new businesses. They are too busy fighting and organizing defense activities. School, work, and entrepreneurship produce investment in the future. Fighting is coercion in the present. The movement of youth from investment in the future to coercion in the present mortgages the economic growth of the future.

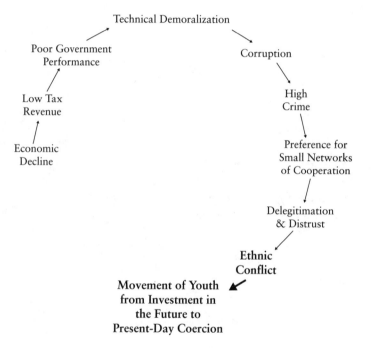

As youth are pulled out of education, society becomes less intellectually capable. With no schooling and no training, there is a decline in skill. With a decline in skill comes a decline in technology and scientific capacity. Put simply, society becomes more stupid. Fundamental engineering, business, and technological skills become lost.

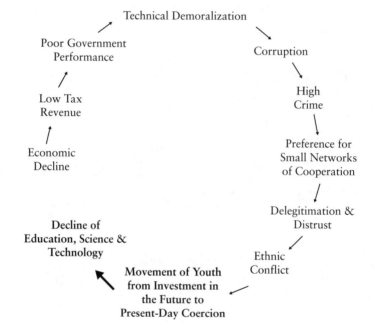

As science and technology languish, projects of large-scale coordination suffer. No one knows how to do anything.

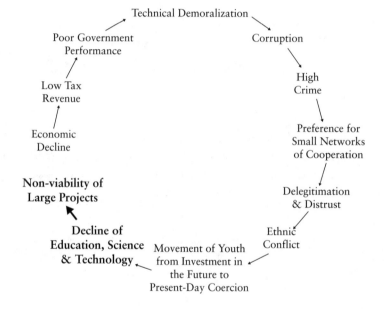

As projects of large-scale coordination become nonviable, economic growth declines. Industry depends on communications, on road building, on scientific progress, on credible financial institutions. As all of these become too difficult to manage, the economy suffers.

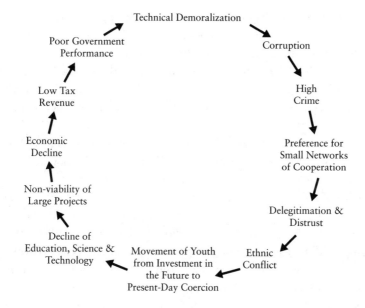

The economic growth declines, making the causal process go full circle. The new economic decline spurs a comparable decline in the other eleven variables in the model. This produces what is known as a *feedback circle*. A decline in one variable causes a decline in all the other variables. The decline in the other variables causes a decline in the original variable. Everything pushes everything to make things systematically worse. There is no brake on the system, so once things start getting worse, they get worse cataclysmically.

Note, however, that the simple circle of death described in the previous figure *understates* the force by which social factors decline. This is because that graph was simplified and only showed causation occurring in one direction.

In fact, every arrow on the graph works in two directions rather than just one. The circle of death also works in reverse. Economic decline kills large projects of joint cooperation simply from budgetary limits. The decline of large projects hurts higher education and education as a whole. As schools get worse, teenagers leave school and turn to activities of present-day coercion. The rise of gangs and militias lead to ethnic conflict. Ethnic conflict leads to delegitimation and preference for small social networks. Delegitimation and hatred of groups outside one's own social network justifies the treatment of these groups as inferiors suitable for rough treatment. This increases the rate of crime. As criminal gangs get richer and more powerful, they are more capable of corrupting the state. Corruption decreases governmental effectiveness. It certainly decreases the capacity of the state to collect taxes. General governmental decline hurts the economy through the non-provision of public goods. The whole process comes full circle again—this time in the opposite direction.

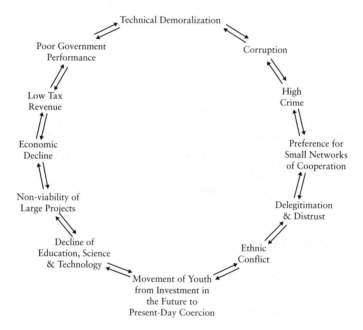

Of course, there is no law that says that the variables in this graph affect only the levels of the variables next to them in the circle. In fact, everything essentially affects everything else. There are 132 sets of relationships in the circle if one allows for everything affecting everything else and in both causal directions.

THE CIRCLE OF SOCIETAL DEATH

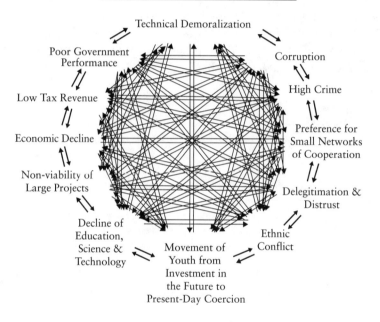

Technical Demoralization

Poor Government
Performance

Corruption

Low Tax Revenue

High Crime

Economic Decline

Preference for
Small Networks
of Cooperation

Non-viability of
Large Projects

Delegitimation &
Distrust

Decline of
Education,
Science &
Technology

Ethnic
Conflict

Movement of
Youth from
Investment in
the Future to
Present-Day Coercion

This means that once something starts going downhill, it can generate very powerful, potent forces of intensification and mutual feedback. This process working in a positive direction explains how there has been such dramatic progress from 1492 to the present day—as all of the variables in the graph were operating in the direction of social amelioration rather than social decline—with massive widespread social improvements in standards of living, peacefulness, crime reduction, legitimation, tolerance, education, and technology. These forces of social improvement were so consistent and so universal that everyone took general improvement to be an entitlement. Of course, economies will grow. Of course, medical technology will improve. Of course, education levels will increase. These were reasonable assumptions given that we had five hundred years of nothing but improvement. The same forces that have operated for the past five hundred years in a positive cycle can also operate in a negative cycle.

The result? Cataclysmic collapse.

Chapter 50

Triggering the Circle
of Societal Death

The Circle of Societal Death is a powerful process. But it is not so powerful if it never gets started. Historically, for the past five hundred to seven hundred years, we have been enjoying a Beneficent Twelve-Step Circle of Societal Growth. This is the same as the Twelve-Step Circle of Societal Decay except that all the forces are moving in a positive rather than a negative direction. In the past few centuries, the economy has been growing. Governments have been well-funded and effective. Corruption is still widespread in some places, but in much of the world it has been essentially cleaned up. Crime is declining. There have been increasing norms of ethnic tolerance. Youth are committing themselves to education. Educational attainment is at all-time high levels as are levels of technological prowess. Never have we been able to do as much in the world as we are capable of doing now.

But it is not hard to trigger the Circle of Societal Death. The previous chapters discussed a number of such potential triggers. The next diagram takes the discussion of those chapters and integrates it visually into the Circle of Societal Death.

There are four possible triggers that could start the Twelve-Step Circle of Societal Death. Note that not every occurrence of every trigger guarantees that a cosmic process of societal decline gets initiated. Everyone knows drunk driving causes accidents. However, many people have too many drinks, get behind the wheel, and get home perfectly safely. Every time a trigger occurs, it puts the world at risk. But the world survives many of these incidents with life going on as normal. That said, here are the kinds of occurrences that *might* start a larger process of global decline.

Declines in the Mensch cycle. Regular downturns in the life cycles of products produce lasting recessions and depressions that are difficult to overcome. The downturns of Mensch cycles are not nearly as adverse for nations in the semiperiphery, which use the distress of the advanced industrial nations to build their own rival manufacturing capacity. But this increases global tensions rather than decreases them, as the populations of the core increasingly view these new emergent nations as existential threats to their own economic well-being. Delegitimation soars because there is little governments can do to produce growth in a down cycle. Politicians turn to militarism and ethnic scapegoating as a tool to deflect popular attention away from their own incapacities to address economic stagnation. Hatred rises. Preference for large networks of cooperation diminishes. Nazism was Germany's response to being on the downturn of a Mensch cycle. Hate groups and protofascism were common in other nations in the 1930s as well. Only the rise of new products and the beginning of a fresh new Mensch cycle based on a new technology can prevent both economies and societies from slipping into a cycle of distrust and decay.

Landlessness. Landlessness leads to political instability. Political instability leads to war. War leads to dislocation and further landlessness. War leads to crime. War leads to ethnic hostility. War draws youth away from education. War destroys economies. War leads to the military control of women by men. The shifting of rural populations from having land to not having land is one of the most potentially destabilizing social changes imaginable.

Ecological collapse. Ecological collapse is bad on its own account. Most traditional end-of-the-world books talk about the possibility of humans

TRIGGERS FOR THE 12 STEP CIRCLE OF SOCIETAL DEATH

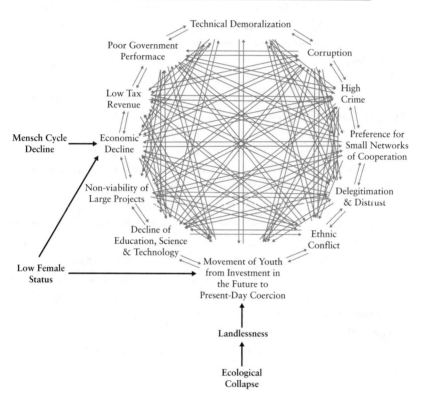

destroying the biosphere. These dangers are real. We could all die from some form of human-induced natural disaster. However, ecological problems are like any other kind of problem. If people work together, they can solve them. The question is whether people will work together.

The neglected aspect of ecological deterioration is what it does to landlessness. As biospheres become ecologically destroyed, the populations of those biospheres become both dispossessed and desperate. This is what is happening with desertification today. The warfare, ethnic hostility, and terrorism we see in Yemen, Afghanistan, Southern Sudan, and Northern Nigeria all have their origins in the desert expanding, destroying the semiarid. The displaced populations have nowhere to go. They are easily recruited by warlords with political agendas.

Saving the semiarid would be easy—simply a matter of introducing birth control, sustainable agriculture, and better wells. None of that is likely if warfare preempts any kind of cooperative rational ecological initiatives.

Increased low female status. Some readers may be skeptical of the role of low female status, given that throughout so much of world history there has been social amelioration while most of the world's women lived under stringent patriarchal regimes. However, high female status is associated with greater female education, greater economic growth from female entrepreneurship, greater women's participation in the economy, and lower fertility creating lower population growth and greater ecological sustainability. Women are more likely to push for better education for their children, causing women's power to be associated with higher levels of education for both sexes. Women have also been instrumental in restarting economies after civil or international wars, with their domestic activities often being the jump start for a revival of agriculture, light manufacture, and commerce. Women are often the force of healing in a world blown apart by male militarism.

~

The world has survived any number of incidents of Mensch cycle decline, land appropriation, ecological decline, and the reduction of women's status. But this does not mean that any of these are intrinsically safe.

The final trigger that ends the modern Euro-American world system may be something that is not on this list. The reader can imagine any number of circumstances that could cause a significant deterioration to one of the twelve variables in the Circle of Societal Death, starting feedback mechanisms with all of the other variables.

But the four triggers listed here are matters of some concern either because they are likely to occur in the foreseeable future or because they are already occurring.

The Mensch cycle based on personal computers and software cannot last forever. At one point, the informatics revolution will come to an end. Silicon Valley will not remain an engine of global growth forever.

The world is currently suffering from an epidemic of new landlessness. Globally, large rural populations are being dislocated as land is purchased or seized for rural or urban development projects. What the free market and paramilitaries cannot accomplish, population growth does, as families have more children than can be sustained by the land.

Desertification and land degradation in general are increasing landlessness. The 2018 *World Atlas of Desertification* estimates that by 2050, up to seven hundred million people will be displaced owing to the destruction of the ecosystem in which they live.

In many nations, there has been a resurgent pushback against the expansion of women's rights. Some of this takes the form of reintroducing limits on abortion. That symbolic indicator is accompanied by attempts to limit women's advancement in the economic sphere. The World Economic Forum's Global Gender Gap report notes that recent years have seen a dramatic reduction in the rate of improvement of many indicators of women's social and economic equality.

Overall, the world is filled with clear and present dangers that could trigger the Twelve-Step Circle of Societal Decay.

Does this mean civilization as we know it has to come to an end?

Not necessarily.

Once processes of societal deterioration have begun, there are ways for people to get together and stop the decay. If people refuse to accept a destruction of global networks of cooperation, then the Beneficent Twelve-Step Circle of Societal Growth could continue.

But just how would people stop a process of social deterioration once it has achieved a solid start?

Chapter 51

CREATING A CULTURE
OF SOCIETAL SURVIVAL

We have now seen the grand historical forces that cause societal decline and fall.

"Grand" historical forces does not mean "inevitable" historical forces.

When many people hear about long-term economic forces or global political forces, they assume these forces are all-powerful.

The macrodynamics are supposedly all backed by giant capitalists that control everything; the economic magnates will buy whatever they need to get what they want. This includes governments and foreign nations. The top elite has choices. You don't.

Or the macrodynamics are based on market forces that have historical inevitability. The free market has its own cycles and its own logic that shape the destiny of the world. There are macroeconomic forces beyond even the ability of central banks to control.

Or the macrodynamics are controlled by all-powerful dictators, warlords, and presidents. The despots will use whatever coercive force they need to get whatever they want. Elections are determined by the big players. The big players are not you.

Or they are backed by centuries of cultural indoctrination. Things have always been this way because people have always been this way. You are not going to change hundreds of years of tradition.

Or they are based on complicated factors that are too difficult to understand. The world is so complex that no one fully understands it or can control it. Nine million independent dynamics are out there, with each person maybe having influence on one mechanism out of the nine million. The complicated mutual interactions are going to lead to unanticipated consequences that will kill us.

Or the world is going to die because too many people would have to agree to get us to change what we are doing and start to fix things. We will never agree because we are too divided. We will die because the world is filled with discord and paralysis.

All of these gloomy scenarios are realistic.

The world really *is* characterized by all-powerful corporate executives, overwhelming market forces, dictators, gangsters, entrenched elected politicians, stubborn people with ideas different from yours, and general all-purpose destructive chaos.

The prognosticators of gloom and doom are realists.

But the presence of all these problems does not mean "game over."

People can choose to let societies die, or they can choose to work to keep things alive. Every society is an aggregation of individual people, and those people are the largest determinants of whether the society prospers or declines. Individual people are the customers to determine what sells and what doesn't. They are the voters and the soldiers that determine what politician wins and what politician loses. They are the creators of the culture they pass on to their friends and their children. If the population is sufficiently stubborn, they can present a CEO or a ruling party with choices that the figures at the top will have to accept.

A society can survive if the people in that society have a culture of survival—a culture that values those things the society needs to grow and that rejects forces that would lead to societal decay. People who have changed their minds and induced other people to change their minds have produced profound effects on world history.

Cultural change is possible.

Some commitments to positive culture have led to enduring improvements in human welfare—even when the objective macro-circumstances looked completely grim.

Chapter 52

CHANGING THE CULTURE OF
ONE-THIRD OF THE WORLD

How Christianity Spread from Palestine

If you want evidence of the ability to produce massive change in global culture, consider the obvious case of the great religions of the world. These nearly always start out small. Hundreds of years later, the views of this small minority have triumphed. How do they accomplish this in the face of such overwhelming odds?

There are three fundamental keys to growth:

1. *Interpersonal contact.* Cultural change occurs person-to-person. People only change their minds on the counsel of people whom they deeply trust. Conversion to a new religion is most likely among people who interact with lots of people in the new religion. Conversion is statistically more probable when the convert is introduced to a missionary by a trusted friend. It is common for spouses of a member of a religion to convert to that religion themselves. Talking to people, building social connections, and creating network ties matter, because this is how one becomes a person of trust.

2. *Having one's religion associated with material success and cultural sophistication.* This is not a matter of spin or marketing. The members of the new religion really *do* have to be wealthy and successful. The members of the new religion really *do* have to be knowledgeable and cool. You can't pretend to be a role model unless you really *are* a role model.

3. *Commitment to proselytization.* Not every religion wants to grow. Some faiths are narrowly concerned with maintaining a comfortable quality of life for preexisting believers. Some religious organizations fear that bringing in new types of people who are different from preexisting members would bring discord or political problems. Concern with a convenient organizational process today can doom a religion to irrelevancy tomorrow. If your religion is not proselytizing, some other religion is. That other religion will grow at your expense.

Readers familiar with the sociology of religion will recognize all the previous ideas as coming from the work of Rodney Stark. Stark has written prolifically about religious conversion in many settings. But his most remarkable work was about the rise of Christianity.

Christianity started as a small Jewish cult in Palestine, on the fringe of the Roman Empire; it was a backwater relative to Greece or Rome itself. It is hard to imagine a world religion coming out of what was an extremely marginal place.

Christianity diffused in an unusual manner. Once Christianity began to spread, it spread in only two directions, west and south.

It expanded west. There were many Christians in Syria, Greece, Rome itself, Sicily, Spain, and North Africa and on the coast of the Black Sea.

It expanded south. The new religion moved down the Nile, where the Sudan and much of the Horn of Africa converted to Coptic Christianity.

It did not expand north. It was not until the 800s that Cyril and Methodius introduced Christianity to Russia and the Slavic regions.

It did not expand east. Mesopotamia and Persia practiced Zoroastrianism in this period. India remained Hindu.

Why did Christianity expand in two directions and not four?

Stark emphasizes the all-important role of Greek merchants. We take merchants for granted in this capitalist era, where they are treated as vulgar businessmen. Merchants were a much bigger deal in ancient times. They could read in a world where most people could not. They traveled widely in a world where most people were peasants who were stuck on one farm. And in a world with no or few stores, they had rare, wonderful, and desirable objects that were unavailable from anyone else. They knew about the cultural doings of faraway places. The merchants were the embodiments of education, sophistication, cosmopolitanism, and the good things of life.

In Palestine, the merchants were Greek. When the Greek merchants adopted Christianity, this was a fantastic opening for growth. It is no accident that the language of the New Testament and early Christian writing was Greek rather than the Aramaic of Palestine. It was the Greeks who were carrying the Christian message to the rest of the world. Greeks traveled all over the Roman Empire. They were respected as emissaries of classical culture everywhere.

Where did the Greeks travel? They traded narrowly within the Roman Empire. The Roman navy patrolled the Mediterranean Sea. Legitimate trade would be protected from pirates. Legitimate trade would be protected from brigands. So commercial convoys could travel by road around the perimeter of the Mediterranean or by sea within the Mediterranean. This also applied to the Roman-controlled Black Sea and its western coast. (The eastern coast was more dangerous.) There was no protection for Greek traders crossing Jordan or Eastern Syria into Mesopotamia. There was no protection for Greek traders in Persia or India.

Technically, there was also no protection for Greek traders who wished to travel up the Nile. However, there were many Greek settlements in Egypt where the Greeks converted the locals to Coptic Christianity. The Egyptians themselves had long-standing trade relationships with the Sudan. This led to further indirect trade relationships with Egyptian traders going to the Horn of Africa. The Coptic Christian merchants took their religion up the river where they received a favorable response.

The merchant story illustrates some of the previous points:

1. The merchants were consummate networkers. Religion follows interpersonal contacts. Trade shapes interpersonal contacts.
2. The success of merchants' proselytization was related both to economic success and cosmopolitanism. Christian merchants were both

spiritual and worldly. They knew of philosophies from faraway places, just as they knew everything else about faraway places.

3. Early Christians knocked themselves out to spread the word about Jesus. They felt they had a better way of life to share. They were not at all shy about sharing it.

The trade and contact factor was really important.
But this, by itself, was not enough.

Chapter 53

CREATING A CULTURE OF CARETAKING

Women in Ancient Rome and 2000's Uganda

It is a substantial accomplishment to become influential and to profoundly change the culture of the world.

It is an even greater accomplishment to create a culture of progress rather than a culture of destruction.

People will adopt cultures that are cultures of caretaking. In hard times, people remember who was good to them and who abandoned them. Religions that grow are religions that help people.

Rodney Stark demonstrated this in his history of early Christianity in the Roman Empire.

Stark argues that Christians took care of people during plagues. Romans did not. This led to an enormous increase in the influence of Christianity.

Ancient cities were beset by epidemics. Sanitation was nonexistent. With no sewers or running water, human and animal waste piled up in the streets. Epidemics struck routinely. When these happened, the Romans had no medical recourse. The mountains were cooler and cleaner than the cities. The healthy Romans evacuated the cities and fled to the mountains. The sick were left behind in the cities to die. Abandonment was the normal fate of a plague patient.

The Christians broke with pagan tradition by intentionally staying behind in plague cities to take care of the victims. They fed them and gave them water. They relieved their fevers as best they could. In no small part, because of the Christians' nursing, many of the otherwise doomed plague patients survived.

Many ex-patients converted to Christianity. The differences between the Romans and the Christians showed the ex-patients exactly who their friends were.

Furthermore, the Christians were modeling behavior that others perceived as admirable. Stark notes Romans encouraged other Romans to be as philanthropic as the Christians. Christians encouraged other Christians *not* to be as un-philanthropic as the Romans. Christians were admired as being kind. They became influential.

There is a gender component to this story.

Converts to Christianity were disproportionately female. Christianity was attractive to women for multiple reasons. In the first place, the Christians banned abortion. Nowadays, the right to have an abortion is a feminist issue. In ancient Rome, the opposite was true. Abortions were ordered by fathers or husbands to be performed on women. Worse, there was no anesthesia. A midwife inserted a sharp instrument into the fully awake woman and began hacking away. Women's right to control her body meant women's right *not* to have a man mutilate her insides just because he felt like it.

The Christians also banned child marriage, a common Roman practice. Eight-year-olds and nine-year-olds were not handed to a man who could do whatever he wanted to them.

Christians allowed widows to live independently without remarrying. Romans did not.

Christians made women religious leaders; a common female title was deacon.

We do not know exactly who provided Christian care to Roman plague victims. However, Christian congregations were heavily female and had many women leaders. It is not much of a stretch to suggest that women were heavily involved in the traditional female role of caregiving.

The role of women in rebuilding societies in duress and re-creating a culture of caring was illustrated by Rae Lesser Blumberg in a comparison of Uganda's and Afghanistan's capacities to recover from civil war. Both Uganda and Afghanistan were ripped apart by extremely violent uprisings—in Uganda, that of the Lord's Resistance Army; in Afghanistan, that of the Taliban. The Lord's Resistance Army was a Christian terrorist group that rose up in Northern Uganda against the national government between 1987 and the 2010s. It was known for the brutality of its tactics. During the war, members of the group abducted over twenty thousand children; mutilation and ritual killings of adults were common.

The Taliban has been trying to gain control of Afghanistan since 1978. It actually ruled from 1996 to 2001 and is still active. The civil war in Afghanistan has killed over 111,000 Afghans, although this figure includes deaths from government action as well.

What happened when these two wars came to an end (or at least a lull in the level of hostilities)? The Northern Ugandan women left the refugee camps and started reconstructing agricultural life in their old villages. They began repairing wells. They began growing crops. Men generally stood aside from agricultural work. So, most of the work involved in regaining self-sufficiency in food and water was done by the women. Because the women were able to leave the camps and operate on their own, recovery in Uganda was relatively rapid.

No such rebound occurred in Afghanistan. Afghanistan was a patriarchal place. Women's activities were controlled. Female education rates were extraordinarily low. Violence against women was routine. Women could only go outside in burkas; Afghan burkas are particularly confining, making physical work extremely difficult. Women could not trade or do business. Under these circumstances, very little of the type of water or agricultural repair that occurred in Uganda occurred in Afghanistan. Economic activity was restricted to men; men were too involved in politics to do much reconstructive agriculture.

Limited economic recovery increased the likelihood of future war. Without viable civilian economic options, working for warlords may be the only way for men to obtain income. Women's reconstruction of an economy is also women's reconstruction of a peace economy. The restriction of women's civilian activities leads to the primacy of war.

The cases of Uganda and Afghanistan are not unique. It appears that women's peacekeeping capacity may be a more general phenomenon. Cross-nationally, women's power—as measured by female labor force participation—is a strong correlate of low levels of civil war and armed conflict. Scholars use female labor force participation as a measure of women's power because it represents how much money is under their control that is not controlled by fathers or husbands. Statistically, in any given nation, for every 5 percent drop in female labor force participation, there is a 500 percent increase in the likelihood of international or civil war. A 500 percent increase in the likelihood of warfare is a lot. A 5 percent change in female labor force participation is not much. I will let the reader speculate on the causal mechanisms behind this relationship.

But giving women economic power seems to do a lot to reduce overall levels of violence.

Chapter 54

CREATING LASTING MEANINGFUL SOCIAL REFORM

The Abolition of Slavery I

It's possible to produce cultural change that produces long-term improvement in human life. People may be suffering because "things have always been done this way." But it is possible to change the culture and stop people from doing things that way.

Consider the case of the abolition of slavery. Slavery or some form of forced labor had been a universal in nearly every society with large-scale agriculture. It was present in China, in India, in most of the regions of precolonial Africa, and in the Aztec and Mayan empires. There was also forced labor in Europe. Russia had serfdom. In Britain, the Master and Servants Act bound workers to particular employers; the forced labor component of this act was not repealed until 1875.

Early attempts to restrict slavery were based on both cynical and idealistic forces. Cynically, reformers wanted to protect people on their own territories from being enslaved. They had fewer objections to making money from slavery in distant places. The English, the French, and the Dutch all banned slavery in their own countries but permitted it in their colonies.

In Britain in the 1700s, however, there arose a small group of reformers who wished to see slavery abolished for all people in all places. The prospects of them succeeding were grim. Britain's economic and military strength was dependent on revenues from sugar colonies. Those colonies used slave labor. Universal abolition was opposed by most of the British ruling class. It was also opposed by the rest of the world.

Yet by 1900, slavery was abolished globally except for a small number of remote outposts. By 1807, Britain had banned the transatlantic slave trade. It had a navy capable of enforcing that ban. In the next century, there were steady abolitions of slavery around the world. The unrealistic dreams of the abolitionists became reality.

Why did this happen? There were both cynical and idealistic factors at work. Cynically, once Britain was committed to abolishing the slave trade, nations that were economically dependent on Britain begrudgingly cooperated. This is what happened in Tunis, in Argentina, in the Ottomans, and with Persia. (The Shah of Iran had to be "encouraged to cooperate" by the British seizing his ships.) Another cynical factor was military. Slaves would be offered manumission in return for fighting in the army of their liberators. This occurred in eighteenth-century French campaigns in the Caribbean and in nineteenth-century civil wars in Latin America.

What matters here, however, is the idealistic factors. In the French Revolution, slavery was banned in French territories as part of *liberté, égalité, et fraternité*. French idealism didn't last. Napoleon, who had little interest in democracy, reestablished the old Caribbean slavery.

British idealism lasted. Britain banned the transatlantic slave trade in 1807. It abolished slavery in all British territories in 1833. These victories were brought about by one of the greatest campaigns in social organizing and ideological persuasion that has ever taken place in human history. Although abolitionist sentiment had existed in Britain long before the great campaigns of the late eighteenth and early nineteenth centuries, the first large wave of popular mobilization against slavery occurred in the 1780s. The Quakers filed the first petition against slavery in 1783. Undoubtedly, the earliest dialogues about abolition involved individual Quakers talking to other Quakers, getting the religion as a whole to stand up against slavery. Having an entire religious denomination committed to abolition mattered. It provided hundreds of pulpits to promote emancipation. It provided a set of natural organizational leaders. It provided large numbers of individuals who would carry the message to other people. It provided money to pay for publications and legal work. Organization matters.

Outreach to other religious groups led to support from Unitarians, Congregationalists, Baptists, and evangelical Anglicans. This led to the formation of the nonsectarian Society for Effecting the Abolition of the Slave Trade. That organization became well-funded and well-staffed.

The next step was the use of mass media. In the 1700s this was an enormous tactical innovation. Having abolitionist petitions printed in as many newspapers as possible provided unheard-of publicity and attracted masses of supporters to their side.

This led to another innovation in British organization: petitions to Parliament based on mass signature campaigns. The first large-scale antislavery petition coming out of Manchester was signed by two-thirds of the city's eligible male voters. Between 1788 and 1807, petitions led to no fewer than thirteen bills for the abolition of the slave trade to be put to the House. This led to constant parliamentary debate.

To be fair, just generating debate was not enough to generate results. Most of the bills that were put forward died. However, the abolitionists were absolutely persistent in the face of defeat. Failed bills just led to even bigger subsequent petitions.

The abolitionists also won because they included women as an integral part of their campaign. Slavery was made a feminist issue involving the exploitation of the bodies of women slaves. Baptist and Methodist abolitionists began to organize all female petitions. In 1833, the year abolition was passed, the largest antislavery petition ever was delivered to Parliament—one with 187,000 signatures, all from women. Four members were required to physically bring the document into the legislative chambers. In the 1832 election, abolitionists got hundreds of candidates to pledge to abolish slavery. Over two hundred of the pledged candidates obtained seats. With that level of electoral organization, abolition became reality.

Social movement organizing and the force of transmission of ideas were fundamental to the elimination of slavery in Britain. Once Britain was committed to the abolition of slavery, it used its economic and diplomatic muscle to obtain reform elsewhere. Brazil, for example, eliminated its participation in the slave trade after the British navy began systematically searching and seizing ships in Brazilian waters. After the Civil War, the United States played this role as well. Cuba abolished slavery in part to avoid giving the United States an excuse to invade under the pretext of emancipating Cuba's slaves.

Chapter 55

CREATING LASTING MEANINGFUL SOCIAL REFORM

The Abolition of Slavery II

Not all emancipations were the result of British or American arm-twisting. Local organization and social movements continued to play a role. Brazil did not emancipate its slaves even after a second British naval assault—a blockade of Rio de Janeiro. What induced Brazil to change? On the one hand, the slaves mobilized themselves. The late nineteenth century saw increasing uprisings by black populations and increasing numbers of organized mass escapes as groups of slaves made runs for the frontier. On the other hand, Brazil urbanized. The urban population had no vested interest in slavery. Abolitionist groups formed in the larger Brazilian cities just as they had formed in Britain. They published newspapers. They organized large demonstrations. They lobbied the Catholic Church for support. (This tactic had mixed results.) They mobilized women.

Local black organizing and urban organizing finally fused. Abolitionists would go out to plantations to facilitate mass flight. They provided free transportation to urban areas and accompanied the slaves to prevent recapture. On arrival, the slaves made common cause with the abolitionists who freed them. This led to bigger demonstrations and more trips to liberate plantations. Soon, army officers were refusing to hunt down fugitive slaves, making the slave laws dead letters. Emancipation legalized what was already a social fact.

Change in public opinion led to the abolition of serfdom in Russia as well. Russia could not be pressured by Britain because its economic ties were to Germany and France. Emancipation was a local movement based on a modernizing elite within the government. Military and civil authorities wanted to see a Russia that was prosperous and militarily capable of competing with more advanced, developed nations. Serfdom posed an obvious military problem, since serfs would side with foreign invaders if they were promised freedom. The Russian elites were also aware that Western Europe was outperforming Russia on every dimension that mattered. If Russia wanted the economy or technology of Western Europe, it would need the modern culture of Western Europe. If that meant free labor, so be it.

So how was abolition achieved?

A small number of people decided the world had to change. They told their story over and over again, recruiting allies from whoever would listen. They connected to institutions of social influence, notably religious organizations and the press. They included otherwise excluded groups. The British and the Brazilians reached out to women. The Brazilians reached out to the slaves themselves. They were politically engaged. The British abolitionists used endless petitions. They elected abolitionist candidates for office. In Russia, the change agents were politically engaged because they were members of the administrative elite themselves.

They were patient. Abolition in Britain, Brazil, and Russia took decades to achieve. In Britain and Brazil, there were frequent setbacks from parliaments and political allies of the slave owners who defeated multiple early versions of reformist legislation. But finally, the victories came and the slaves were freed.

This story is not devoid of geopolitical realities. It did not hurt that Britain was the most powerful nation in the world and that it was able to impose its will on others through either economic threats or military sanctions. Nineteenth-century Serbia would have had a harder time achieving a global transformation of labor relations.

But there were also moral and ideological elements that helped win the battle as well. Abolitionist movements existed in many of the countries that were being pressured by Britain. And Britain was helped by having the highest standard of living in the world—making progressives who wanted to improve the quality of life in their own nation look to Britain as a benchmark example.

Achieving global social change is a difficult task. It is possible, but it takes patience and global mobilization. However, sometimes keeping everything from unraveling requires local commitment and local action in times of crisis when everything is looking dark.

The antislavery campaign involved creating new and unprecedented forms of progress. What happens when the forces of good are on the defensive and what matters is protecting the progress that has already been made?

Chapter 56

Doing the Right Thing under
Impossible Conditions

Saving the Jews under Nazism

Saving the world is not easy. Never mind the difficulty of communicating positive ideas in a world of negativity. Sometimes stepping up is downright dangerous. In a world of collapsing law and order, gangs and criminal cartels rule. In a world of decreasing tolerance and increased scapegoating, ethnic violence is prevalent. Standing up to do the right thing may get you killed.

But people really do stand up to do the right thing even when doing so puts them in great peril. The best example is rescuing Jews in Nazi Europe. Opposing the Nazis or opposing Nazi sympathizers was obviously extremely dangerous. But many, many Europeans did this. The World Holocaust Remembrance Center has identified nearly twenty-seven thousand people who put their lives at risk by rescuing Jews. It is difficult to know exactly how many Jews were saved by these heroes, but it is undoubtedly a large number. Most of the eight thousand Jews in Denmark were saved; estimates of Jewish survivorship in the Netherlands range between seven thousand and sixteen thousand; fifty thousand Bulgarian Jews were saved; fifty thousand to one hundred thousand Jews in Poland were saved.

It is easy to be cynical and think that one person or one small group cannot make a difference. But in these cases, individual people and individual small groups made all of the difference in the world. Their actions were extremely consequential, even when the rest of the world was bent on murderous destruction.

What distinguished the people who became rescuers from those people who did not?

1. Rescuers Were Nonconformists
2. They Did Not Just Do What Everyone Else in Their Country Was Doing
3. They Were Agenda Makers Rather than Agenda Takers
4. And Their Agendas Changed the World Around Them

Nechama Tec interviewed a large number of rescuers in Poland. The biographies of these rescuers were highly diverse. People came to rescuing through a wide variety of personal routes. But one personality characteristic unified most of the rescuers. They were all individualists. They did not blend in with other people around them. Other researchers have claimed these people were marginal. Most of Tec's evidence comes from interview quotes showing rescuers as fairly cantankerous:

From Rescuers Themselves
"I was always an individualist. I had my special circle which was made up of theosophists. I don't eat meat. . . . I am different from other people but this does not bother me."

"I am an individualist, a cat who moves on his own road. I have always had a special and individual . . . approach to things which is different from the way others do."

"I pay too little attention to what others think. . . . I say things that others would not say."

From Survivors Who Observed Rescuers
"[My rescuer] did not fit into her environment at all. She was very different. People accepted her . . . and looked up to her. But she was an outsider."

"[My rescuers] were more than strange. They were weird. [One] never washed ever! . . . They were completely isolated."

"She was an oddball. Different."

They operated with limited amounts of social support, but they were okay with that. Their independence gave them the willingness to ignore the majority when it was in the wrong. Their isolation bought them privacy that facilitated their not being noticed by the authorities.

Working as a deviant individual could be good. Working as a deviant group was probably better. Robert Braun has found that in the Netherlands, rescue work was concentrated among religious minorities. In Protestant regions of the Netherlands, Catholics did the rescuing. In Catholic regions of the Netherlands, Protestants did the rescuing.

Why were minority religionists more likely to step up and take altruistic action?

Much of the same logic applied in the Netherlands as applied in Poland. The members of the smaller religion were accustomed to disagreeing with their neighbors—and thus maintained the courage of their own convictions.

However, belonging to a church meant they had an entire social network of people they could trust. They could coordinate joint activities far beyond the capacity of a single individual to arrange. They could get other people to cover for them. They had allies who would protect them from danger. They could pool money and material resources. They could try out new ideas on willing listeners who could protect them from first-draft misconceived schemes.

The minority religionists operated as a team. Teams can do more than individuals.

Did the European rescuers completely neutralize fascism and bring about a new peaceful post-Nazi era?

No.

The future of Europe was to be determined by the dynamics of World War II and by the military and economic capacities of the various geopolitical powers.

But the culture of destruction ended, at least during the war, in the houses and churches of the rescuers. Individuals willing to be different made a difference. Groups willing to be different were able to make an even bigger difference.

Chapter 57

What You Can Do to Save the World

Okay, the world is going to fall apart at some stage.

It is entirely possible that it will start falling apart during our lifetimes.

What can we do to prevent this from happening, or stop the process once it has begun?

Remember, massive cultural change *is* possible. The assumption that there is nothing individuals can do to change historical forces is simply wrong. No one thought that the religion of one-third of the world's people would come from an obscure outpost on the edge of the Roman Empire. No one thought that slavery—a fact of life for two thousand years—would be abolished.

So how do you change the culture of a world on a downward slide?

1. *Dialogue. Talk to as many people as you can.*

   When networks of trust and cooperation are shrinking, people only talk to people in their own social circle. New ideas are scarce. People on the other side get caricatured.

Reaching out and talking to other people that one would not otherwise talk to is key. Sharing new ideas helps build trust and confidence. There really are good human beings on the other side of the fence.

And remember, dialogues are not monologues.

The benefits of getting together and talking come from not only sharing your great ideas about the world but also listening to others and learning from them as they share their stories.

2. *Maintain a positive message about the importance of global cooperation and working together.*

People have to be reminded about the power of large social networks and what has been achieved in the past when everyone built something together. It's a story that needs to be told over and over and over again.

Yes, everyone usually likes "working together" in principle. However, they hate cooperating with horrible people who can't be trusted. The challenge is to identify areas of common interest. The hope is to get people to admit (even grudgingly) that at least on this one issue, the two groups might be natural allies. The other side may not be "okay" in general, but they might be "okay" in this one case. It's a start.

3. *Eliminate intolerance.*

Note that some people who think they are really, really tolerant— Really aren't.

If you distrust people of the other political faction, or you distrust people who have treated people like yourself poorly, you might have turned into a very biased person. Eliminating intolerance is a two-way proposition. The first step toward eliminating discrimination in others is to eliminate it in oneself.

4. *Maintain a positive message about the importance of science and education.*

Education, science, and technology are how we are going to solve the great problems of the world. Mensch cycle decline is not an issue if we can invent new and fantastic products that can be the basis of a new Mensch cycle and economic renewal. We can't save the planet through ecological modernization if we don't have the scientific base to make technological environmental fixes.

5. *Maintain a positive message about the state and taxation.*

Many of the key solutions to national problems really will come from big government. Yes, the private sector will help too. However, if solving a social problem is not particularly profitable, then the government will be the main force for coming up with a solution while absorbing the financial loss. Saving the world from plague is not particularly profitable if it means giving drugs to people who can't pay for them. But if you want to stop a plague, someone has to cover the bill. The government is good at covering those bills.

Taxes are what makes government effective and honest. Remember that an underfunded government is both an ineffective government and a corrupt government.

If you don't like big government now, you will like it even less when it goes corrupt.

6. *Provide real assistance to the people in your world.*

Lasting long-term commitments are more meaningful here than one-shot holiday gestures.

7. *Women Are Powerful Carriers of Positive Social Messages.*

Social change is a two-gender operation. On many key issues, women have led the way.

8. *Become a multiethnic global citizen.*

Go everywhere. Talk to everyone. Have a web of relationships that crosses every possible line.

9. *Rich people and corporations are not the enemy.*

One of the things that need saving is the economy. Profit-making companies are the forces that build the economy.

It is also possible to forget that businesspeople are human beings too. They have a sense of justice. They have a sense of fairness. They know when the world is going awry. They want to save the world as much as you do.

It will be firms that turn around the Mensch cycle and firms that do the actual work of ecological modernization.

In the most important dialogues about saving the planet, many of the key participants will be people wearing suits.

10. *Cynicism is the enemy.*

If we are cynical and skeptical, it is highly unlikely that we will be able to accomplish anything impressive.

Cynicism feels smart because you are supposedly smart enough to know everything that is wrong with every plan. Only a sophisticated person like you can see how something is going to fail.

In fact, cynicism is a form of stupidity.

Cynicism happens when you cannot figure out a solution to a problem. You become an engineer without a clue.

Anyone can look at a problem and shrug their shoulders.

Only the deepest understanding of the causes of a problem will provide a way for that problem to be solved.

You cannot eliminate cynicism in other people until you eliminate cynicism in your own mind.

You cannot overcome the problem of helplessness until you overcome the problem of helplessness in your own mind.

A great Japanese philosopher once said:

Hope is a decision.

Appendix

Unit of Analysis Issues in Comparative Social Science

This book is meant for a general readership. Therefore, I finesse some methodological issues that are of interest to academic social scientists. If critics who care about those technical issues wish to raise objections, they will find me guilty as charged. I simplify my exposition in the interest of clarity to nonacademic readers. Too many social scientists seem to think they are writing exclusively for their dissertation advisers; in doing so they fail to tell their story to the world.

The primary point I punted on was the unit of analysis question in macrosocial science. The book is titled *How Societies Die*. Technically, there is no such thing as a society. There are *nation-states*. There are *empires*. There are *oikumenes*. There are *oiekeioses*. There are *interactional civilizations*. There are *world systems*. There are *cultural civilizations*. Each of these has different properties and a different life span and requires a different theory to deal with it.

A *nation-state* is a government that enjoys a monopoly of coercive force within its territory. It is what we think of when we think about a country. The United States is a nation-state, as are France and Canada. Its borders are measured by the applicability of its laws. On the American side of Niagara Falls, US law prevails. Cross the border to the other side, Canadian law prevails. A nation-state can fall without completely disrupting the social, economic, or cultural institutions associated with it. Montenegro has been part of many nation-states during its history, including some periods where it was its own country. It remained basically Montenegro. Note that many present-day nations do not enjoy an absolute monopoly of coercive power within their own borders. In the most recent Colombian civil war, much of the southern part of that country was ruled by a rebel group: FARC.

An *empire* is a political unit that influences territories beyond its borders by the use of coercive force. The rule of law may or may not extend to these extraterritorial regions. The influence of the center may ebb and flow with time. But the empire has the power to mobilize resources and impose its will on outlying units. Note that both the United States and France are clearly empires; Canada can act in this manner on occasion. A nation can maintain its sovereign integrity but lose most or all of its imperial power. Spain has far less of its imperial power today than it did in 1550.

An *oikumene* is a set of market relations. The United States does business all over the globe. Some of this business involves independent nations, such as China, where the United States has no legal power at all. The borders of the ancient Roman oikumene were far, far larger than those of the empire. Rome traded all over Europe, had extensive bilateral relationships with Persia, and through Persia had substantial trade relations with Han China. I place very great weight on both national and global economies as sources of human well-being. Understanding such market relations is critical to questions of rise and fall.

An *oikos* is a relation between organized human behavior and the environment. Many of the resources that humans acquire are obtained through trade or production. Thus, the oikumene captures some of what is in an oikos. However, a nontrivial proportion of human energy use comes from sources that are not associated with a society in any manner whatsoever. Humans extract fish from the open sea. Humans mine or cut down timber in unincorporated territories in areas that may or may not be inhabited. For ecological theory, it is generally the oikos that matters.

An *interactional civilization* is a set of nation-states that have multiplex relationships that incorporate political, economic, and cultural aspects. Europe generally has been an interactional civilization.

A *world system* is an interactional civilization where a set of strong nations at the core exploits a set of weaker nations in the periphery. Both groups advance, but the core advances more than the periphery. Most of the important empires and interactional civilizations have taken the form of a world system. Our modern world today is best described as a world system dating from the middle 1300s in which Western Europe's exploitation of Eastern Europe and the Eastern Mediterranean gave way to substantial extraction of wealth from Latin America. The core expanded to North America and Japan. The periphery expanded to the rest of the world. A large semiperiphery emerged in an intermediate status of exploitation.

A *cultural civilization* is what people think of when they think of *civilization*. It is a set of ideas, values, and artistic productions that are admired and preserved. The Roman Empire may have fallen; however, Roman civilization is alive and well. We still build buildings using Roman models. One-third of the world practices a Roman religion, Christianity, the former state religion of Rome. Principles of Roman law guide Western law, which is in turn practiced in much of the world. We still study classical philosophy and entertain ourselves with stories of Greek gods and heroes. Confucian values have been a long-standing feature of northeastern Asian life, despite the Chou dynasty falling over two thousand years ago. When people bemoan the fall of Western civilization, they are often bemoaning the fall of Western values. Culture, however, seems to last long after the societies that produced those values have faded from existence.

Picking any of these units of analysis would have required concentrating on a smaller subset of variables, picking a different set of dates for rises and falls, and generating theories that may or may not resemble the theories presented here. Each of the units of analysis would have required a different theory.

Scholars who concentrate on a particular unit of analysis are openly invited to generate their own theories. The theories presented here are a starting point for a larger analysis.

Most of those new treatments will require some analysis of the global economy, some analysis of the financial integrity of the state, some analysis of violence, and some analysis of legitimation. I suspect the elements of this book will not be useless to people building newer, more finely grained theories.

Scholarly References

Chapter 1

The dates for Rome, Byzantium, China, and Egypt are fairly standard.

The 1492 date for the rise of the West comes from Wallerstein, Immanuel. 1980. *Modern World System I: Capitalist Agriculture and the Rise of the European World-Economy in the Sixteenth Century*. New York: Academic. Wallerstein sees the discovery of the Americas and the infusion of Mexican and Peruvian silver into the European monetary supply as the sparkplug event that generated the modern growth process.

Angus Maddison, the leading econometrician of the history of world economic growth, argues that there was dramatic growth between 1000 and 1500 in Western Europe. See Maddison, Angus. 2007. *Contours of the World Economy, 1-2030 AD*. New York: Oxford. Most growth curves are geometric, so the lion's share of that growth would have occurred in the latest third of that period.

On growth in medieval Europe in general, see Pirenne, Henri. 2014. *Economic and Social History of Medieval Europe*. Eastford, CT: Martino.

Chapter 2

My basic arguments on Rome all come from Ward-Perkins, Bryan. 2005. *Fall of Rome and the End of Civilization*. New York: Oxford University Press.

For an example of the rosy view of the early Middle Ages that Ward-Perkins was refuting, see Brown, Peter. 1971. *World of Late Antiquity*. New York: Norton.

On the economic woes of Late Byzantium, see Laiou, Angeliki. 2008. *Economic History of Byzantium*. Washington, DC: Dumbarton Oaks.

Chapters 3 and 4

Most of this discussion closely follows Laiou, Angeliki, and Cecile Morrisson. 2007. *Byzantine Economy*. New York: Cambridge University Press. The Plethon quote can be found on page 192 of this source.

Chapter 5

Both the African and Middle Eastern map are adapted from Peel, M. C., Finlayson, B. L., and McMahon, T. A. 2007. "Updated world map of the Köppen-Geiger climate classification." *Hydrol. Earth Syst. Sci.* 11: 1633–1644, https://doi.org/10.5194/hess-11-1633-2007. I express gratitude to Michael Bechthold for his preparation of these excellent maps.

On the expansion of the semiarid, see Huang, Jianping, Mingxia Ji, Yongkun Xie, Shanshan Wang, Yongli He, and Jinjiang Ran. 2015. "Global Semi-arid Climate Change over Last Sixty Years." *Climate Dynamics* 46:1131–1150; and Cherlet, M., C. Hutchinson, J. Reynolds, J. Hill, S. Sommer, and G. von Maltitz, eds. 2018. *World Atlas of Desertification*. Luxembourg: Publication Office of the European Union.

Chapter 6

Theda Skocpol's main argument about fiscal crises in the French can be found in Skocpol, Theda. 1979. *States and Social Revolutions: Comparative Analysis of France, Russia and China*. New York: Cambridge.

For data on the rising cost of war, see Rasler, Karen, and William Thompson. 1989. *War and Statemaking: Shaping of the Global Powers*. Boston: Unwin Hyman, particularly chapter 5, 119–154.

Chapters 7 and 8

The basic argument presented here comes from Mohamoud, Abdullah. 2006. *State Collapse and Post-conflict Development in Africa: Case of Somalia (1960–2001)*. Lafayette, IN: Purdue University Press. This is an utterly extraordinary book and I cannot recommend it highly enough to readers interested in African affairs.

The GDP statistics are from the Angus Maddison dataset. "Maddison Project Database." Groningen Growth and Development Centre. https://www.rug.nl/ggdc/historical development/maddison/. 2018.

The fatality statistics are from Mohamoud 2006, 16.

The piracy statistics are from Daniels, Christopher. 2012. *Somali Piracy and Terrorism in the Horn of Africa*. Plymouth, UK: Scarecrow.

On the size of the refugee population, see Mohamoud 2006, 123–126.

On what little of the Somali economy survived after the crash, see Little, Peter. 2003. *Somalia: Economy without State*. Oxford: International African Institute in conjunction with Indiana University Press.

On piracy as a defensive reaction against international threats, see Weldemichael, Awet Tewelde. 2019. *Piracy in Somalia: Violence and Development in the Horn of Africa*. New York: Cambridge University Press.

On the international response to Somali piracy, see Daniels 2012, chapter 4.

On the extent of contemporary violence, see the 2020 Human Rights Watch Report on Somalia. https://www.hrw.org/world-report/2020/country-chapters/somalia.

Chapter 10

For a well-argued, popular view of societal fall due to environmental catastrophes, see Diamond, Jared. 2005. *Collapse: How Societies Choose to Fail or Succeed*. New York: Penguin. This is also the source for the first three ecological collapses listed in the table.

On Mesopotamia, see Jacobsen, Thorkild and Robert Adams. 1958. "Salt and Silt in Ancient Mesopotamian Agriculture." *Science* 128: 1251–1258.

Within social science, such models are referred to as "treadmill of production" models. A good review of treadmill of production models and their alternatives can be found in Givens, Jennifer, Brett Clark, and Andrew Jorgenson. "Strengthening the Ties between Environmental Sociology and the Sociology of Development." In *Handbook of the Sociology of Development*, edited by Gregory Hooks, 69–94. Berkeley: University of California Press.

Famous statements of the treadmill of production model include Foster, John Bellamy, Brett Clark, and Richard York. 2010. *Ecological Rift*. New York: Monthly Review; and Schnaiberg, Allan. 1980. *Environment*. New York: Oxford University Press.

For a review of the evidence on global warming, see NASA's website on the issue. https://climate.nasa.gov/evidence/.

For a discussion of the causes and effects of population growth, see Weeks, John. 2015. *Population: An Introduction to Concepts and Issues*. Boston: Cengage. Chapter 2 contains a discussion of global population projections and why growth continues to occur. Chapter 11 discusses the ecological consequences of population growth.

For another treatment of ecological consequences of population growth, see Brown, Lester, Gary Gardner, and Brian Halweil. 1999. *Beyond Malthus: Nineteen Dimensions of the Population Challenge*. New York: Norton.

On Mesopotamia, see Weiss, H., A. Courty, W. Wetterstrom, F. Guichard, L. Senior, R. Meadow, and A. Curnow. 1993. "Genesis and Collapse of Third Millennium North Mesopotamian Civilization." *Science* 261 (5124): 995–1004.

On ecological modernization, see Mol, Arthur. 2001. *Globalization and Environmental Reform*. Cambridge, MA: MIT Press.

For the related literature on sustainable development, see Elliot, Jennifer. 2013. *Introduction to Sustainable Development*. New York: Routledge.

Chapter 11

There are many moral crisis books. Among them are the following: Gibbon, Edward. 2020. *The History of the Decline and Fall of the Roman Empire*. Lambertville, NJ. Maven Books; Spengler, Oswald. 2006. *Decline of the West*. New York: Vintage; Black, Jim Nelson. 1994. *When Nations Die: Ten Warning Signs of a Culture in Crisis*. Carol Stream, IL: Tynedale; Schultz, Kenneth. 2017. *Decline and Imminent Fall of the West*. Privately published.
For the more nuanced approach of Paul Collier, see Collier, Paul. 2018. *The Future of Capitalism: Facing the New Anxieties*. New York: Harper Collins.
On the low level of crime in contemporary America, see the "Criminal Victimization 2018," *National Crime Victimization Survey*. Department of Justice: Bureau of Criminal Statistics. https://www.bjs.gov/index.cfm?ty=dcdetail&iid=245. 2019.

Chapters 12–15

Parsons is not easy reading. The Wiki articles on him and on AGIL are good, although the personal page overemphasizes biography at the expense of his theory. See "Talcott Parsons". *Wikipedia*. https://en.wikipedia.org/wiki/Talcott_Parsons; 8/18/2020 and "AGIL Paradigm". *Wikipedia*. https://en.wikipedia.org/wiki/AGIL_paradigm. 8/18/20.
Readers who want to read original works are advised to start with Parsons, Talcott. 1964. "Evolutionary Universals in Society." *American Sociological Review* 29:339–357, which is a short, basic introduction to his theory. The fuller model can be found in Parsons, Talcott. 1970. *Social System*. London: Routledge and Kegan Paul.
On size and empires, see Eisenstadt, Shmuel N. 1963. *Political System of Empires*. Glencoe, IL: Free Press.
On the role of religious tolerance in early Swiss economic history, see Capitani, Francois de. 1986. "Vie et Mort de l'Ancient Regime 1648–1815." In *Nouvelle Histoire de la Suisse et des Suisses*, edited by Jean Claude Favez, 423–496. Lausanne: Payot Lausanne; and Bergier, Jean-Francois. 1983. *Histoire de la Economie de la Suisse*. Lausanne: Editions Payot. Unfortunately, English-language treatments of this issue are not as detailed. See Church, Clive, and Randolph Head. 2013. *Concise History of Switzerland*. New York: Cambridge University Press, for a short treatment.
The concept of greater and lesser self can be found in Ikeda, Daisaku. 2001. *For the Sake of Peace: Seven Paths to Global Harmony—a Buddhist Perspective*. Santa Monica, CA: Middleway.

Chapter 16

On GDP 1820–2010, see Bolt, Jutta, Marcel Timmer, and Jan Luiten van Zanden. 2014. "GDP per Capita since 1820." Pp. 57–72 in *How Was Life? Global Well-Being since*

1820, edited by Jan Luiten van Zanden, Joerg Baten, Marco Mira d'Ercole, Auke Rijpma, Conal Smith, and Marcel Timmer. Paris: OECD. https://doi.org/10.1787/97892 64214262-en.
On calories per capita, see Vasileska, Angela, and Gordana Rechkoska. 2012. "Global and Regional Food Consumption Patterns and Trends." *Procedia—Social and Behavioral Sciences* 44:363–369.

Chapter 17

The statistics on life expectancy come from Luiten van Zanden, Jan, Joerg Baten, Marco Mira d'Ercole, Auke Rijpma, Conal Smith, and Marcel Timmer. 2014. *How Was Life? Global Well-Being since 1820*. Paris: OECD. Updated versions of these statistics can be found on the Clio Infra website, https://clio-infra.eu/.
The discussion of determinants of historical changes in mortality is a standard one in demography. A good introduction to the subject is provided by Weeks, John. 2015. *Population: An Introduction to Concepts and Issues*. Boston: Cengage.

Chapter 18

The statistics in the table come from Eisner, Manuel. 2003. "Long Term Historical Trends in Violent Crime." *Crime and Justice: A Review of Research* 30:83–142.
For an extended and high-quality discussion of the Eisner findings and data from parallel sources, see Pinker, Steven. 2011. *Better Angels of Our Nature: Why Violence Has Declined*. New York: Viking.
For a more reserved treatment that also covers the rise and fall of crime observed in non-Western settings, see Baten, Joery, Winny Bierman, Peter Foldvari, and Jan Luiten van Zanden. 2014. "Personal Security since 1820." In *How Was Life? Global Well-Being since 1820*, edited by Jan Luiten van Zanden et al., 139–158. Paris: OECD.
On highwaymen, see Appleby, John, and Paul Dalton, eds. 2009. *Outlaws in Medieval and Early Modern England: Crime, Government and Society c. 1066—c. 1600*. New York: Routledge; Sharpe, J. A. 1984. *Crime in Early Modern England, 1550–1750*. London: Longman; Schreiber, Hermann. 1962. *Merchants, Pilgrims and Highwaymen: A History of Roads throughout the Ages*. London: Putnam.
Pirates are also covered in the general crime discussions above. But for more specific treatments, see Chet, Guy. 2014. *Ocean Is a Wilderness: Atlantic Piracy and the Limits of State Authority 1688–1856*. Amherst: University of Massachusetts Press; Wadsworth, James. 2019. *Global Piracy: Documentary History of Seaborne Banditry*. London: Bloomsbury Academic.
For a classic discussion of both types of crime as Robin Hood–style acts of class warfare, see Hobsbawm, Eric. 1969. *Bandits*. London: Weidenfeld and Nicholson.
The rise of courts as a method of peaceful conflict adjudication is covered as a significant side topic in Stone, Lawrence. 1972. *Causes of the English Revolution: 1529–1642*. New York: Routledge.

One can find general discussions of the causes of crime in most criminology textbooks. For a good one, see Siegel, Larry. 2017. *Criminology: Theory, Patterns and Typologies*. Boston: Cengage.

On greater cosmopolitanism and kinder treatment of strangers, see Pinker 2011; and also Elias, Norbert. 1939. *Civilizing Process*. Cambridge, UK: Blackwell.

Chapter 19

The basic account of raiding follows the first third of volume 1 of Mann, Michael. 1986. *Sources of Social Power*. New York: Cambridge University Press.

The gender component comes from Lerner, Gerda. 1986. *Creation of Patriarchy*. New York: Oxford University Press.

Chapter 20

Marx's discussion of primitive accumulation can be found in Marx, Karl. 2011. *Das Kapital*. Scotts Valley, CA: Createspace. Volume 1, part 8, chapter 26.

The theory that capitalist economic growth is grounded in agricultural export is known as staples theory. The primary work was done in Canada by Innis, Harold. 1933. *Problems of Staples Production in Canada*. Toronto: Ryerson; and Watkins, M. H. 1963. "Staple Theory of Economic Growth." *Canadian Journal of Economics and Political Science* 29:141–158.

The compelling general statement of the position with evidence from around the world is Senghaas, Dieter. 1985. *European Experience: Historical Critique of Development Theory*. Dover, NH: Berg.

On the American case, see Cochrane, Willard. 1979. *Development of American Agriculture: Historical Analysis*. Saint Paul: Minnesota University Press; and McMichael, Philip. 2013. *Food Regimes and Agrarian Questions*. Rugby, UK: Practical Action.

There is no unified general discussion at the global scale of the role of the proletarianization of indigenous people as a precondition for the expansion of capitalism. This is a marked gap. For a good collection of essays on the phenomenon in various nations limited to ranching rather than agriculture, see Adhikari, Mohamed, ed. *Genocide on Settler Frontiers: When Hunter Gatherers and Commercial Stock Farmers Clash*. New York: Berghahn. For the United States, see Dunbar-Ortiz, Roxanne. 2014. *Indigenous People's History of the United States*. Boston: Beacon. For Canada, see Dickason, Olive Patricia. 1997. *Canada's First Nations: History of Founding People from Early Times*. Toronto: Oxford University Press.

The master theorist of capitalist expansion through the incorporation of space is David Harvey. See Harvey, David. 2019. *Spaces of Global Capitalism: Theory of Unequal Geographical Development*. London: Verso.

On primitive accumulation in Colombia, see Hristov, Jasmin. *Paramilitarism and Neoliberalism: Violent Systems of Capital Accumulation in Colombia and Beyond*. London: Pluto. Further support for Hristov's argument can be found in Richani, Nazih. 2002. *Sys-*

tems of Violence: Political Economy of War and Peace in Colombia. Albany: State University of New York Press.

Chapter 21

The basic argument presented here is known as dependency theory. The classic statement of dependency theory is Frank, Andre Gunder. 1978. *Dependent Accumulation and Underdevelopment.* London: Macmillan. The Frank exposition is garrulous and twisting. For a later, simpler, and more straightforward account, see Elsenhans, Harmut. 1984. *Development and Underdevelopment: History, Economics and Politics of North-South Relations.* Thousand Oaks, CA: SAGE.

On Indonesia, see Geertz, Clifford. 1963. *Agricultural Involution: Processes of Ecological Change in Indonesia.* Berkeley: University of California Press.

On India, see Prabhakara, M. P. 1990. *Historical Origin of India's Underdevelopment: World System Perspective.* Lanham, MD: University Press of America.

On the role of tariffs in preserving manufacture in Europe and the lack of same destroying manufacture in India, see Chang, Ha-Joon. 2008. *Bad Samaritans: Myth of Free Trade and the Secret History of Capitalism.* London: Bloomsbury; and Reinert, Erik. 2007. *How Rich Countries Got Rich and Why Poor Countries Stay Poor.* New York: Public Affairs.

The chapter's final argument about Japan comes from the closing chapter of Geertz 1963.

Chapter 22

On the behavior of American multinationals in Latin America in the 1960s, see Barnet, Richard, and Ronald Muller. 1975. *Global Reach: Power of the Multinational Corporation.* New York: Cape. Note that Barnet and Muller's statistics underestimate the contribution of American corporations to the assets of subsidiaries by assigning all depreciation to the share of resources contributed by the locals. The figures presented in this book correct for Barnet and Muller's bias by assigning depreciation between American and local sources in the same ratio as was reported for original seed investments.

On five years of higher growth followed by fifteen years of lower growth, see Bornschier, Volcker, and Christopher Chase-Dunn. 1985. *Transnational Corporations and Underdevelopment.* New York: Praeger; and Kentor, Jeffrey. 1998. "Long Term Effects of Foreign Investment Dependence on Economic Growth: 1940–1990." *American Journal of Sociology* 103:1024–1046.

On the chaotic findings concerning the effect of foreign direct investment on growth in more contemporary settings, see Alframji, Mohammad Amin, and Mahmoud Khalid Almsafir. 2013. "Foreign Direct Investment and Economic Growth: A Literature Review from 1994 to 2012." *Procedia—Social and Behavioral Sciences* 129:206–213.

Chapter 23

On global long-term cycles of debt, see Suter, Christian. 1992. *Debt Cycles in the World-Economy: Foreign Loans, Financial Crises and Debt Settlement.* New York: Routledge; and Reinhart, Carmen, and Kenneth Rogoff. 2009. *This Time Is Different: Eight Centuries of Financial Folly.* Princeton, NJ: Princeton University Press.

For long-term Latin American debt cycles, see Marichal, Carlos. 1989. *Century of Debt Crises in Latin America.* Princeton, NJ: Princeton University Press.

On the Egyptian debt crisis of the nineteenth century, see Owen, E. R. J. 1969. *Cotton and the Egyptian Economy, 1820–1914: Study in Trade and Development.* Oxford: Clarendon; Landes, David. 1958. *Bankers and Pashas: International Finance and Economic Imperialism in Egypt.* New York: Harper Torchbook; Ezzelarab, Abdel Aziz. 2002. *European Control and Egypt's Traditional Elites: Case Study in Elite Economic Nationalism.* Lewiston, NY: Edwin Mellen; and Toussaint, Eric. 2016. "Debt as an Instrument of the Colonial Conquest of Egypt." Committee for the Abolition of Illegitimate Debt. http://www.cadtm.org/spip.php?page=imprimer&id_article=13562.

On the most recent Latin American debt crisis, see Potter, George Ann. 2000. *Deeper Than Debt: Economic Globalization and the Poor.* London: Latin American Bureau; and Chossudovsky, Michel. 1998. *Globalisation of Poverty: Impacts of IMF and World Bank Reforms.* London: Zed.

Chapter 24

The arguments in this chapter invoke a standard theory in development sociology: the theory of the developmentalist state. A basic exposition can be found in Wade, Robert. 1990. *Governing the Market: Economic Theory and the Role of Government in East Asian Industrialization.* Princeton, NJ: Princeton University Press.

On Korea, and on developmentalist states in general, see Amsden, Alice. 1989. *Asia's Next Giant: South Korea and Late Industrialization.* New York: Oxford.

On Japan, the classic discussion is Johnson, Chalmers. 1982. *MITI and the Japanese Miracle: Growth of Industrial Policy, 1925–75.* Stanford, CA: Stanford University Press.

For the adaptation of the Korean model to China, see Walder, Andrew. 2005. "Local Governments as Industrial Firms: An Organizational Analysis of China's Transitional Economy Source." *American Journal of Sociology* 101:263–301.

Chapter 25

I have written extensively on the state and development. See Cohn, Samuel. 2016. "State and Economic Development." In *Handbook of Development Sociology*, edited by Gregory Hooks, 393–412. Berkeley: University of California Press; and Cohn, Samuel. 2012. "O'Connorian Models of Peripheral Development—or How Third World States Resist World Systemic Pressures by Cloning the Policies of States in the Core." Pp. 336–344 in *Handbook of World Systems Analysis*, edited by Salvatore Babones and Christopher Chase-Dunn. New York: Routledge. For a book-length discussion, see Cohn, Samuel. 2012. *Employment and Development under Globalization: State and Economy in Brazil*. Basingstoke, UK: Palgrave Macmillan.

My ideas were heavily drawn from O'Connor, James. 1973. *Fiscal Crisis of the State*. New York: St. Martin's; Wade, Robert. 1990. *Governing the Market: Economic Theory and the Role of Government in East Asian Industrialization*. Princeton, NJ: Princeton University Press, and a general literature on the relative efficacy of states and markets in generating economic growth. For a fine set of essays on this theme, many of which are synergistic with my thinking, see Putterman, Louis, and Dietrich Rueschemeyer, eds. 1992. *State and Market in Economic Development*. Boulder, CO: Lynne Rienner.

Chapter 26

My Brazil study is *Employment and Development under Globalization*. 2012. Basingstoke, UK: Palgrave Macmillan.

The two Kasarda studies showing that airports increase the economic growth of American cities in which they are located are Irwin, Michael, and John Kasarda. 1991. "Air Passenger Linkages and Employment Growth in U.S. Metropolitan Areas." *American Sociological Review* 56:524–537; and Kasarda, John, and David Sullivan. 2006. "Air Cargo, Liberalization, and Economic Development." *Annals of Air and Space Law* 31:214–230.

On the history of Hartsfield Airport, see Braden, Betsy, and Paul Hagan. 1989. *Dream Takes Flight: Hartsfield International Airport and Aviation in Atlanta*. Athens: University of Georgia Press; and Hartsfield, Dale. 2014. *What's in a Name? Historical Perspective of Hartsfield-Jackson Atlanta International Airport*. Scotts Valley, CA: Createspace.

On the role of Heathrow in the growth of Southeastern England, see Massey, Doreen. 1974. *Towards a Critique of Industrial Location Theory*. London: Center for Environmental Studies.

Chapter 27

Most of this chapter is drawn from Cole, Jonathan. 2009. *The Great American University: Its Rise to Preeminence, Its Indispensable National Role, Why It Must Be Protected*. New York: Public Affairs.

On the balance of basic research between universities and industry, see the Science Coalition, "Federal Government and U.S. Research Universities: Driving Innovation That Fuels the Economy." http://www.sciencecoalition.org/downloads/1392650077b asicresearchandtheinnovationprocess.pdf. Accessed 8/18/2020. Its figures show that in 2009, industry did only 20 percent of basic research in the United States. Universities and the federal government did 65 percent of the basic research. Well over 80 percent of industrial research and development was in the commercial development of established technologies, rather than in basic or applied research into new technologies. The federal government and universities themselves provided the overwhelming majority of the funding for basic research.

Chapter 28

The data in this chapter come from Bank of Boston. 2003. *Engines of Economic Growth: The Impact of Boston's Eight Research Universities on the Metropolitan Boston Area*. New York: Appleseed. www.masscolleges.org/files/downloads/economicimpact/EconomicReport _Rull%20Report_Final.pdf.

Chapter 29

The data on nations that have cut taxes come from Lundeen, Andrew. 2014. "Every OECD Country Except the U.S., Chile, and Hungary Has Lowered Its Corporate Tax Rate since 2000." Tax Foundation, August 20, 2014. https://taxfoundation.org /every-oecd-country-except-us-chile-and-hungary-has-lowered-its-corporate-tax -rate-2000/. In the time since this article was published, the United States has lowered its rates too. See also the OECD Global Revenues Statistics Database at http://oe.cd /global-rev-stats-database.

The full James O'Connor citation is O'Connor, James. 1973. *Fiscal Crisis of the State*. New York: St. Martin's.

On tax avoidance by large American corporations, see "Profitable Companies, No Taxes. Here's How They Did It." *New York Times*, March 9, 2017. https://www.nytimes.com /2017/03/09/business/economy/corporate-tax-report.html.

On the class basis of Tea Party participation, see Skocpol, Theda, and Vanessa Williamson. 2016. *Tea Party and the Making of Republican Conservatism*. New York: Oxford University Press.

Note that this chapter somewhat ignores the role of white racism and anti-immigration sentiment in producing support for conservatives. Those issues are not trivial; they are addressed in the chapters on ethnic hostility. However, the transition to Reaganism and hostility toward Bill Clinton were probably driven more by the Tea Party's tax agenda than by nativism. Since then, anti-immigration forces and antistate forces have combined. This is what makes for the power of both Trumpism and neo-populist movements in Europe.

Chapter 30

On investors investing overseas after the Bush tax cut, see Congressional Research Service. 2012. *U.S. Direct Investment Abroad: Trends and Current Issues*. Washington, DC: Congressional Research Service.

On the two contradictory effects of tax increases in microeconomic theory, see Musgrave, Richard. 1959. *Theory of Public Finance: Study in Public Economy*. New York: McGraw

Hill; Stiglitz, Joseph. 1969. "Effects of Income, Wealth and Capital Gains Taxation on Risk Taking." *Quarterly Journal of Economics* 83:262–283.

On American firms responding to taxation, see Vroman, Wayne. 1967. "Macroeconomic Effects of Social Insurance." PhD dissertation, Department of Economics, University of Michigan.

On Moroccan firms responding to taxes, see Currie, Janet, and Ann Harrison. 1997. "Sharing the Costs: Impact of Trade Reform on Capital and Labor in Morocco." *Journal of Labor Economics* 15: S44–S71.

On the extent of tax evasion, see Bird, Richard. 1992. *Tax Policy and Economic Development*. Baltimore: Johns Hopkins University Press.

On large American companies that legally pay no taxes whatsoever, see Strachan, Maxwell, and Alissa Scheller. 2014. "These 26 Companies Pay No Federal Income Tax." *Huffington Post*, February 26, 2014. www.huffingtonpost.com/2014/02/25/corporation-tax-rate_n_4855763.

On the causes of the death of firms, see Ames, Michael. 1983. *Small Business Management*. New York: West.

On the state of the statistical evidence on the effect of tax cuts on growth, see Wasylenko, Michael. 1997. "Taxation and Economic Development: State of the Economic Literature." *New England Economic Review*. Federal Reserve Bank of Boston (March/April): 37–52.

For partisan conservative reviews of the literature that shows tax cuts leading to strong job creation, see the work of the Tax Institute. For partisan liberal reviews of the literature that shows tax cuts having no effect whatsoever, see the work of the Economic Policy Institute. Wasylenko 1997 provides a balanced review of the literature from both sides.

Chapter 31

The statistics on murder come from the "Murder Rate By Country." *World Population Review*. https://worldpopulationreview.com/countries/murder-rate-by-country/. Accessed 8/18/2020.

On the weakness of kidnapping statistics, see Briggs, Rachel. 2001. *Kidnapping Business*. London: Foreign Policy Centre.

The data on State Department kidnapping warnings comes from CNN. "State Department Warns Americans of Kidnapping Risk in 35 Nations Including Parts of Africa and Mexico." April 11, 2019. https://www.cnn.com/2019/04/10/politics/state-depart ment-travel-advisory-kidnapping-risk/index.html.

The Mexican kidnapping statistics come from Smith, Rory. 2018. "Hundreds of People in Mexico Are Getting Kidnapped Every Year. And the Problem Is Getting Worse." *Vox*, May 11, 2018. https://www.vox.com/2018/5/11/17276638/mexico-kidnappings -crime-cartels-drug-trade.

The Pernambuco kidnapping statistics come from Guerra, Raphael. 2019. "Casos de Sequestro Relampago Aumentam 41% em Pernambuco" [Cases of rapid-strike kidnapping went up 41% in Pernambuco]. *Jornal do Comercio*, February 22, 2019. https://jc .ne10.uol.com.br/colunas/ronda-jc//2019/02/21/casos-de-sequestro-relampago

-aumentam-41-em-pernambuco/. The São Paulo statistics come from "Casos de Se-
questro Relampago Aumentam 30% em São Paulo" [Cases of rapid-strike kidnapping
went up 30% in São Paulo]. *Globo*, June 28, 2017.
The materials in the table on Brazilian kidnappings came from Lista10. 2019. "10 Maiores
Sequestros Que Chocaram o Brasil" [Ten greatest kidnappings which shocked Brazil].
August 21, 2019. https://lista10.org/diversos/10-maiores-sequestros-que-chocaram-o
-brasil/. Lista10 is a website that features a lot of Top 10 lists in Portuguese.
On the shutdown of Rio de Janeiro, see Penglase, Ben. 2005. "Shutdown of Rio de Ja-
neiro: Poetics of Drug Trafficker Violence." *Anthropology Today* 21 (5): 3–6.
On the Tim Lopes story, see the Wikipedia page for Tim Lopes. "Tim Lopes". Wiki-
pedia. https://en.wikipedia.org/wiki/Tim_Lopes. Accessed 8/18/2020. The Wiki page
does not cover the government backdown from the investigation.
There is no English-language account of the attacks on the Shopping Rio Sul or city hall;
Portuguese-language accounts of those attacks can be found in the newspapers *Jornal do Brasil* and *O Globo*.

Chapter 32

The primary argument in this chapter is adapted from the work of Desmond Arias. The
most important statement of his position can be found in Arias, Desmond. 2006. *Drugs
and Democracy in Rio de Janeiro: Trafficking, Social Networks and Public Security*. Cha-
pel Hill: University of North Carolina Press. A more recent statement that extends
the argument to non-Brazilian settings can be found in Arias, Desmond. 2018. *Criminal Enterprises and Governance in Latin America and the Caribbean*. New York: Cambridge University Press.
Technically, Arias does not like the use of the term "parallel power" because he uses that
term to refer to the secondary government being all gangs while the government itself is squeaky clean. He was one of the early writers to document the role of corrupted
police in the alternative governance process.
I include militias and ex–police officers as members of the criminal element and incorporate them into the term. For a militia-based parallel power discussion similar to
mine with very convincing evidence on how much power and control the new militias
have, see Wheeler, Joanna. 2014. "Parallel Power in Rio de Janeiro: Coercive Media-
tors and Fragmentation of Citizenship in the Favela." In *Mediated Citizenship: Informal Politics of Speaking for Citizens in the Global South*, edited by Bettina von Lieres
and Laurence Piper, 93–109. Basingstoke: Palgrave Macmillan.
On the de facto impunity of both rogue police and death squads in Brazil, see Intera-
merican American Commission on Human Rights. 1997. "Police Violence, Impunity
and Exclusive Military Jurisdiction for the Police." Chapter 3 of *Report on the Situation of Human Rights in Brazil*. Washington, DC: Organization of American States.
http://www.cidh.org/countryrep/brazil-eng/chaper%203.htm. See also Human Rights
Watch. 2009. "Lethal Force: Police Violence and Public Security in Rio de Janeiro and
São Paulo." https://www.hrw.org/report/2009/12/08/lethal-force/police-violence-and
-public-security-rio-de-janeiro-and-sao-paulo.

For a current discussion of militias, including the multiple links of Brazil's president Bolsonaro to the militias, see Wheatley, Jonathan. 2019. "Rio de Janeiro's Militias: A Parallel Power in Bolsonaro's Brazil." *Financial Times*, March 24, 2019. https://www.ft.com/content/bdd61718-4b10-11e9-bbc9-6917dce3dc62.

On catch and release, see Arias 2006.

For an application of these ideas to how criminal warlords get power in Africa, see Reno, William. 2010. "Persistent Insurgencies and Warlords: Who Is Nasty, Who Is Nice and Why?" In *Ungoverned Spaces: Alternatives to State Authority in an Era of Softened Sovereignty*, edited by Annie Clunan and Harold Trinkunas, 57–76. Stanford, CA: Stanford University Press.

Chapter 33

For an encyclopedic discussion of ways people morally justify corruption, see Prasad, Monica, Mariana Borges da Silva, and Andre Nickow. 2019. "Approaches to Corruption: Synthesis of the Scholarship." *Studies in International Comparative Development* 54:96–132. This review identifies no fewer than 260 scholarly articles that discuss local cultural framings of corruption; those articles are listed in a helpful bibliography at the end.

Chapter 34

The technical demoralization concept is my own. However, my thinking was heavily shaped by Theobald, Robin. 1990. *Corruption, Development and Underdevelopment*. Durham, NC: Duke University Press, notably chapter 4.

Chapter 35

For an exhaustive and detailed review of the many cleanup procedures that have been tried in the Global South, see Gans-Morse, Jordan, Mariana Borges, Alexey Makarin, Theresa Mannah, Blankson, Andre Nickow, and Dong Zhang. 2018. "Reducing Bureaucratic Corruption: Interdisciplinary Perspectives on What Works." *World Development* 105:177–188. They are clear about identifying limitations to the reforms they describe, although they do identify real short-term successes.

On the clean-up in Great Britain, see Gladden, Edgar Norman. 1967. *Civil Services of the United Kingdom: 1855–1970*. Norman, UK: Cass.

On the clean-up in Singapore, see Quah, Jon S. T. 2016. "Singapore's Success in Combating Corruption: Four Lessons for China." *American Journal of Chinese Studies* 23:187–209.

Chapter 36

The distinction I am making between ethnic hostility based on enduring cultural differences and hostility based on the exploitation of situations for economic advantage is referred to as *primordial* versus *instrumental* models of ethnicity in the literature. For a discussion of the difference between the two and the analytical superiority of the instrumental model, see Henderson, Errol. 1999. "Ethnic Conflict and Cooperation." In *Encyclopedia of Violence, Peace and Conflict*, edited by Lester Kurtz, 751–764. New York: Academic.

On middleman minorities, see Bonacich, Edna. 1973. "A Theory of Middleman Minorities." *American Sociological Review* 38 (October): 583–594. For a recent application to Jews, see Grosfeld, Irena, Seyhun Orcan Sakalli, and Ekaterina Zhuravskaya. 2020. "Middleman Minorities and Ethnic Violence: Anti-Jewish Pogroms in the Russian Empire." *Review of Economic Studies* 87:289–342. For an application to anti-Chinese violence in Southeast Asia, see Chua, Amy. 2002. *Worlds on Fire: How Exporting Free Market Democracy Leads to Ethnic Hatred and Global Instability*. New York: Anchor.

On the imposition of serfdom in Eastern Europe, see Wallerstein, Immanuel. 1980. *Modern World System I: Capitalist Agriculture and the Rise of the European World-Economy in the Sixteenth Century*. New York: Academic. On the imposition of forced labor in Indonesia, see Geertz, Clifford. 1963. *Agricultural Involution: Processes of Ecological Change in Indonesia*. Berkeley: University of California Press.

The cheap labor argument is fairly obvious. Readers seeking scholarly versions of this position can try Harris, Donald. 1979. "Capitalist Exploitation and Black Labor: Some Conceptual Issues." *Review of Black Political Economy* 8:133–151; Coalson, George. 1952. "Mexican Contract Labor in American Agriculture." *Southwestern Social Science Quarterly* 33:228–238; or White, Anne. 2017. *Polish Families and Migration since EU Accession*. New York: Polity.

On Sunni-Shia conflicts in Iraq, see Wehrey, Frederic M. 2013. *Sectarian Politics in the Gulf: From the Iraq War to the Arab Uprisings*. New York: Columbia University Press.

On the Rwandan war, see Berry, Marie. 2018. *War, Women and Power: From Violence to Mobilization in Rwanda and Bosnia-Herzegovina*. New York: Cambridge University Press.

On Nigeria, see Suberu, Rotimi. 1999. *Ethnic Minority Conflicts and Governance in Nigeria*. Lagos: Spectrum.

Chapter 37

This chapter is drawn nearly entirely from Lange, Matthew. 2012. *Educations in Ethnic Violence: Identity, Educational Bubbles and Resource Mobilization*. New York: Cambridge University Press.

Chapter 38

The landlessness model presented here comes from Paige, Jeffery. 1978. *Agrarian Revolution: Social Movements and Export Agriculture in the Underdeveloped World*. Glencoe, IL: Free Press.

Chapter 39

The best cross-national study of the landlessness–political instability relationship by far is Thomson, Henry. 2016. "Rural Grievances, Land Inequality and Civil Conflict." *International Studies Quarterly* 60:511–519. What sets this study apart is that the author does not look merely at land holdings and calculate a Gini coefficient (inequality statistic) for the size of plots, which is traditional practice. The Gini Index for plot sizes does not measure what percentage of the population is actually landless. Thomson takes the rural population and calculates their distribution on the land, including who has zero land whatsoever.

Older, less reliable studies include Binswanger, Hans, Klaus Deininger, and Gershon Feder. 1995. "Power, Distortions, Revolt and Reform in Agricultural Land Relations." In *Handbook of Development Economics*, edited by Jere Behrman and T. N. Srinivasan, 2659–2772. Amsterdam: Elsevier (which found that landlessness causes political instability); and Collier, Paul, and Anke Hoeffler. 2004. "Greed and Grievance in Civil War." *Oxford Economic Papers* 56:563–595 (which found that it does not).

On Pakistan, see Malik, Sadia Mariam. 2011. "Empirical Investigation of the Relationship between Food Insecurity, Landlessness and Violent Conflict in Pakistan." Pakistan Institute of Development Economics Working Paper 2011:71, Pakistan Institute of Development Economics, Islamabad.

On the Movimento Sem Terra mobilizations of landless workers in Brazil, see Albertus, Michael, Thomas Brambor, and Ricardo Ceneviva. 2018. "Land Inequality and Rural Unrest: Theory and Evidence from Brazil." *Journal of Conflict Resolution* 62:557–596. Unlike Thomson, Albertus, Brambor, and Ceneviva view landlord self-defense as inconsistent depending on the degree to which protest is viewed as a threat. For general background on the Sem Terras, see Wolford, Wendy. 2010. *This Land Is Ours: Social Mobilization and the Meanings of Land in Brazil*. Durham, NC: Duke University Press.

On landlessness and rural violence in Colombia, see Albertus, Michael, and Oliver Kaplan. 2013. "Land Reform as a Counterinsurgency Policy: Evidence from Colombia." *Journal of Conflict Resolution* 57198–231; and Richiani, Nazih. 2014. *Systems of Violence: Political Economy of War and Peace in Colombia*. Albany: State University of New York Press.

On post–World War II Sumatra, see Pelzer, Karl. 1957. "Agrarian Conflict in East Sumatra." *Pacific Review* 30:151–159.

On contemporary Sumatra, see Subilhar, Rosmery, and Husnul Isa Harahap. n.d. "Agrarian Conflict in the North Sumatera: The Hopes and Progress." https://eudl.eu/pdf/10.4108/eai.5-9-2018.2281292. Accessed 8/18/2020.

On the Arab Spring in Tunisia, see Gana, Alia. 2012. "The Rural and Agricultural Roots of the Tunisian Revolution: When Food Security Matters." *International Journal of the Sociology of Agriculture and Food* 19:201–213.

For other empirical material, see the statistical analysis and case studies in Jeffery Paige's original *Agrarian Revolution*; the collection of essays on land conflicts around the world in Moyo, Sam, and Paris Yeros. 2005. *Reclaiming the Land: Resurgence of Rural Movements in Africa, Asia and Latin America*. London: Zed; and the bibliography in Bruce, John. 2013. "Land and Conflict: Land Disputes and Land Conflicts." USAID Issue Brief, United States Agency for International Development, Washington, DC. https://

www.land-links.org/wp-content/uploads/2013/06/USAID_Land_Tenure_Land _and_Conflict_Issue_Brief_1.pdf

Chapter 40

The land transaction data can be found at "All Deals" Land Matrix Public Database. https://landmatrix.org/data/. 2020.
On violent land grabs in Colombia, see Hristov, Jasmin. *Paramilitarism and Neoliberalism: Violent Systems of Capital Accumulation in Colombia and Beyond.* London: Pluto.
On the more consensual (but still problematic) land sales of India, see Levien, Michael. 2018. *Dispossession without Development: Land Grabs in Neoliberal India.* New York: Oxford University Press.

Chapter 41

World population size estimates, projections, and fertility statistics are from the United Nations World Population Prospects, United Nations Department of Social and Economic Affairs. More specifically, population size estimates and projections can be found in the dataset "Total Population—Both Sexes." https://population.un.org/wpp /Download/Standard/Population, 2019.
Fertility statistics can be found in the dataset "Crude Birth Rates." https://population .un.org/wpp/Download/Standard/Fertility, 2019.

Chapters 43 and 44

For a simple introduction to Mensch and Kondratieff cycles, see Berry, Brian, Edgar Conkling, and D. Michael Ray. 1987. *Economic Geography: Resource Use, Locational Choices and Regional Specialization in the Global Economy.* Englewood Cliffs, NJ: Prentice Hall. Chapter 11.
Berry et al. is also the source of the waves listed in the table. The details concerning the end of the fourth wave and the birth of the fifth wave are my own additions, since these occurred after the 1987 publication date of the book.
For diehards who have to read authors in the original, see Kondratieff, Nikolai. 1935. "Long Waves in Economic Life." *Review of Economic Statistics* 17:105–115; and Mensch, Gerhard. 1983. *Stalemate in Technology: Innovations Overcome the Depression.* New York: Harper Collins.
For technical econometric debates over K cycles, see Goldstein, Joshua. 1988. *Long Cycles: Prosperity and War in the Modern Age.* New Haven, CT: Yale University Press. Chapter 3. The debate did not stop there.
On long-term international transfers of technology and their implications for global competition, see Amsden, Alice. 2001. *Rise of the Rest: Challenges to the West from Late-Industrializing Economies.* New York: Oxford University Press.

Chapter 46

On the Jason Moore model of expanding frontiers, see Moore, Jason. 2015. *Capitalism in the Web of Life: Ecology and the Accumulation of Capital.* London: Verso. A predecessor of the expanding frontiers model was developed by Stephen Bunker. See Bunker, Stephen, and Paul Ciccantell. 2005. *Globalization and the Race for Resources.* Baltimore: Johns Hopkins University Press.

On the Rios Montt massacres, see Burt, Jo-Marie, and Paulo Estrada. 2018. "The Legacy of Ríos Montt, Guatemala's Most Notorious War Criminal." International Justice Monitor, April 2, 2018. https://www.ijmonitor.org/2018/04/the-legacy-of-rios-montt -guatemalas-most-notorious-war-criminal/; and Rios Montt's obituary in the *New York Times*, April 1, 2018. https://www.nytimes.com/2018/04/01/obituaries/efrain-rios-montt -guatemala-dead.html.

On the adverse effects of war on development, see Hooks, Gregory. 2016. "War and Development in the Twenty-First Century." *Blackwell Encyclopedia of Sociology.* https:// doi.org/10.1002/9781405165518.wbeos0870.

Chapter 47

The ideas and material in this chapter come from Blumberg, Rae Lesser. 2016. "Magic Potion / Poison Potion: Impact of Women's Economic Empowerment versus Disempowerment for Development in a Globalized World." In *Sociology of Development Handbook*, edited by Gregory Hooks, 153–189. Berkeley: University of California Press.

Chapter 48

For the Leicht and Baker argument on declining male status, see Leicht, Kevin, and Phyllis Baker. 2019. "Gender through the Looking Glass: Role of Low Status Men in the Reproduction of Global Gender Violence and Racial and Ethnic Bigotry." Pp. 175–188 in *Gender and Development: Economic Basis of Women's Power*, edited by Samuel Cohn and Rae Lesser Blumberg. Thousand Oaks, CA: SAGE.

For the Blumberg and Cohn argument on war, see "Power of the Purse: Importance of Women's Economic Power: Why Women's Economic Power Is Absolutely Essential." In *Gender and Development: Economic Basis of Women's Power*, edited by Samuel Cohn and Rae Lesser Blumberg, 1–27. Thousand Oaks, CA: SAGE.

On antifeminism in Poland, see Snitow, Ann, and Kathryn Detwiler. 2016. "Gender Trouble in Poland." *Dissent.* https://www.dissentmagazine.org/article/gender-trouble -poland-pis-abortion-ban.

On women in Yemen, see the unusually good Wiki article on the topic. "Women in Yemen." *Wikipedia.* https://en.wikipedia.org/wiki/Women_in_Yemen. Accessed 8/18/2020.

On backlash against quotas for women parliamentarians in Kenya, see Berry, Marie, Yolande Bouke, and Marilyn Muthoni Kamuru. 2020. "Implementing Inclusion: Gender

Quotas, Inequality and Backlash in Kenya." *Politics and Gender.* https://doi.org/10.1017 /S1743923X19000886.

On femicide in Turkey, see "440 Women Were Murdered and 317 Women Were Sexually Assaulted." Kadin Cinayetlerini Durduracagiz Platformu [We Will Stop Women's Murders Platform]. http://kadincinayetlerinidurduracagiz.net/veriler/2870/440-women -were-murdered-and-317-women-were-sexually-assaulted. Accessed 8/18/2020.

On Central American gender violence, see Walsh, Shannon, and Cecilia Menjívar. 2016. "Impunity and Multisided Violence in the Lives of Latin American Women: El Salvador in Comparative Perspective." *Current Sociology* 64:586–602; and Walsh, Shannon, and Cecilia Menjívar. 2017. "Architecture of Feminicide: State, Inequalities and Everyday Gender Violence in Honduras." *Latin American Research Review* 52:221–240.

On femicides in Argentina, see Zambrano, Adriana Marisel. n.d. "Informes de Femicidio en Argentina" [Information on femicide in Argentina]. La Casa del Encuentro. http://www.lacasadelencuentro.org/femicidios03.html. Accessed 8/18/2020.

On legislative changes in women's status in Argentina, see Htun, Mala. 2003. *Sex and the State: Abortion, Divorce and the Family under Latin American Dictatorships and Democracies.* New York: Cambridge University Press.

On online antifeminism in Argentina, see Engler, Veronica. 2017. "Antifeminismo Online." *Nueva Sociedad* 269 (May–June). https://nuso.org/articulo/antifeminismo-online/.

The statistics on global violence against women come from the United Nations Office on Drugs and Crime. 2019. *Global Study on Homicide: Gender-Related Killings of Women and Girls.* Vienna, United Nations.

Chapters 52 and 53

The full reference for Rodney Stark's sociological history of early Christianity is Stark, Rodney. 1996. *Rise of Christianity: A Sociologist Reconsiders History.* Princeton, NJ: Princeton University Press.

The argument about the directionality of Christianity's spread comes from volume 1 of Mann, Michael. 1986. *Sources of Social Power.* New York: Cambridge University Press.

On the prevalence of epidemics in ancient settings, see McNeill, William. 1976. *Plagues and Peoples.* Garden City, NJ: Doubleday.

Stark's claim of high female status is controversial, although I endorse it. For a supporting view, see Blainey, Geoffrey. 2011. *Short History of Christianity.* New York: Viking. Counterviews, such as Reuther, Rosemary Radford. 1982. "Feminism and Patriarchal Religion: Principles of Ideological Critique of the Bible." *Journal for the Study of the Old Testament* 7:55–62, tend to base themselves on antifeminist texts in Christian writings rather than on empirical observations by contemporary writers about what Christians of the time actually did.

The full reference to the analysis of Northern Uganda and Afghanistan is Blumberg, Rae Lesser. 2016. "A Walk on the Wild Side of Gender, War and Development in Afghanistan and Northern Uganda." In *Development in Crisis: Threats to Human Well-Being in the Global North and the Global South*, edited by Rae Lesser Blumberg and Samuel Cohn, 134–154. Abingdon, UK: Routledge.

For a quick introduction to the Lord's Resistance Army, see "Q and A on Joseph Kony and the Lord's Resistance Army." *Human Rights Watch*. https://www.hrw.org/news /2012/03/21/qa-joseph-kony-and-lords-resistance-army. 3/12/2012.

Casualty counts for the Afghan civil war come from "Civilian Casualties in the War in Afghanistan." *Wikipedia*. https://en.wikipedia.org/wiki/Civilian_casualties_in_the _war_in_Afghanistan_(2001%E2%80%93present). Accessed 8/18/2020.

On the trade-off between civil war and the robustness of the civilian economy, see Collier, Paul, V. L. Elliott, Anke Hoeffler, Marta Reynol-Querol, and Nicholas Sambanis. 2003. *Breaking the Conflict Trap: Civil War and Development Policy*. Washington, DC: International Bank for Reconstruction and Development.

On the role of gender inequality in reducing armed conflict, see Caprioli, Mary. 2005. "Primed for Violence: The Role of Gender Inequality in Predicting Internal Conflict." *International Studies Quarterly* 49:161–178.

Chapters 54 and 55

Most of the material here comes from Seymour Drescher's magisterial review of the global history of slavery. Drescher, Seymour. 2009. *Abolition: A History of Slavery and Antislavery*. New York: Cambridge University Press.

On slavery in precolonial Africa, see Lovejoy, Paul E. 2011. *Transformations of Slavery: A History of Slavery in Africa*. New York: Cambridge University Press.

On slavery in Asia and the New World, see Rodriguez, Junius. 1996. *Historical Encyclopaedia of Slavery*. Santa Barbara, CA: ABC-CLIO.

On forced labor in Britain, see Steinberg, Marc. 2016. *England's Great Transformation: Law, Labor and the Industrial Revolution*. Chicago: Chicago University Press.

On the British abolition campaign, see Hochschild, Adam. 2006. *Bury the Chains: The British Struggle to Abolish Slavery*. London: Pan.

On the role of organizations in successful social movements, see McCarthy, John, and Mayer Zald. 1977. "Resource Mobilization and Social Movements: A Partial Theory." *American Journal of Sociology* 82:1212–1241; or Oberschall, Anthony. 1972. *Social Conflict and Social Movements*. Englewood Cliffs, NJ: Prentice-Hall. Oberschall features extensive documentation on religious organizations.

On the abolition of serfdom in Russia, see Stansziani, Alessandro. 2016. "Abolition of Serfdom in Russia. In *Abolitions as a Global Experience*, edited by Hideaki Suzuki, 228–255. Singapore: National University of Singapore; and Lincoln, W. Bruce. 1982. *In the Vanguard of Reform: Russia's Enlightened Bureaucrats, 1825–1861*. De Kalb: Northern Illinois University Press.

Chapter 56

The primary material for this chapter comes from Braun, Robert. 2019. *Protectors of Pluralism: Religious Minorities and the Rescue of Jews in the Low Countries during the Holocaust*. New York: Cambridge University Press; and Tec, Nechama. 1986. *When*

Light Pierced the Darkness: Christian Rescue of Jews in Nazi-Occupied Poland. New York: Oxford University Press.

The estimate of the number of rescuers comes "Righteous Among the Nations Database." Yad Vashem World Holocaust Remembrance Center. https://righteous .yadvashem.org/. Accessed 8/18/2020.

The survivorship statistics are from chapter 1 of Tec 1986.

On the marginalism thesis, see London, Perry. 1970. "Rescuers: Motivational Hypotheses about Christians Who Saved Jews from Nazis." In *Altruism and Helping Behavior*, edited by Leonard Berkowitz and J. Macaulay, 241–250. New York: Academic.

Chapter 57

The final quote is the closing line of Ikeda, Daisaku. 2006. *Determination*. Santa Monica, CA: Middleway.

Appendix

The distinctions made here draw from David Wilkinson's schemata that he first laid out in his 1987 "Central Civilization." *Comparative Civilizations Review* 17:31–59 and reiterated in his two-part 1992/1993 "Cities, Civilizations and Oikumenes." *Comparative Civilizations Review* 27:51–87 and 28:41–74. I avoid his "universal empire" and "state systems" categories, which seem to be subsets of "interactional civilizations." Wilkinson carefully disassociated himself from the cultural interpretation of the word "civilization," leading to the "interactional civilization" language given here. The cultural interpretation is analytically useful and reflects what most people mean when they discuss civilization. So, I added that category back into the analysis.

On world systems, see Wallerstein, Immanuel. 1974. *Modern World System*. Vol. 1. New York: Academic.

The term "oikeos" was introduced in Jason Moore's 2013 "From Object to *Oikeios*: Environment Making in the Capitalist World Ecology." http://citeseerx.ist.psu.edu /viewdoc/download?doi=10.1.1.691.5540&rep=rep1&type=pdf and is repeated in his later works, such as the 2015 *Capitalism and the Web of Life*. London: Verso.

On long-distance across-boundary trade, see Curtin, Philip. 1984. *Cross-Cultural Trade in World History*. New York: Cambridge University Press.